eccentric EDINBURGH

J.K. GILLON

MOUBRAY HOUSE PUBLISHING

EDINBURGH 1990

FOR EMMA JANE

As a native of Larbert — famed for its toffee production and concentration of psychiatric hospitals — James 'Jack' Gillon had early acquaintance with the idiosyncratic. It was a taste he developed during spells of employment as a street photographer, student psychiatric nurse, Peat Stooker, Butlin's Redcoat and, now, a member of the Historic Buildings Section in Edinburgh's Planning Department.

Jim Crumley, who introduces this book, is fondly remembered for his perceptive and witty features in the *Edinburgh Evening News*. His publications include *The Royal Mile* (Moubray House, 1989).

ECCENTRIC EDINBURGH
Text © James K Gillon 1990

Published by Moubray House Publishing Ltd.
Tweeddale Court, 14 High Street
Edinburgh EH1 1TE

Cover designed by Scott Y Doran
Book designed by Dorothy Steedman
Production by Nic Allen
Electronic page make-up by Alison Bird
Printed by Billings Bookplan, Worcester

A CIP catalogue record for this book is available from The British Library

ISBN 0 948473 18 5

eccentric
EDINBURGH

CONTENTS

JOHNNIE DOWIE, from the *Scots Magazine*, 1806

INTRODUCTION

Eccentric? Edinburgh? The two words sit as ill-at-ease in the same breath as 'Knox' and 'Mary'. Is it not, after all, the case that the city has been straight-jacketed by that turbulent preacher's legacy — cool, undemonstrative and gray? This emotionally-stifling domain has provided the butt of a limitless store of 'you'll-have-had-your-tea' jokes and other sidewipes so beloved of generations of Glasgow music hall comedians, and we all know how many a true word there must be in so much jest.

Is it possible, then, that the sense of liberated individuality which breeds eccentricity could ever have taken root in such a seedbed of conformity? Could such an inhibited city really breed enough eccentricity to fill both sides of a tram ticket to Corstorphine, let alone a whole book?

The myth of Edinburgh as a place of well-ordered gentility and correctness which represses the natural spirit and vitality of her citizens is certainly tenacious. But consider this:

'Beautiful as she is, she is not so much beautiful as interesting. She is pre-eminently Gothic, and all the more so since she has set herself off with some Greek airs and erected classic temples on her crags. In a word, and above all, she is a curiosity.'

Or this:

'There is a spark among the embers; from time to time the old volcano smokes. Half a capital and half a country town, the whole city leads a double existence; it has long trances of the one and flashes of the other.'

Or this:

'. . . trumpets may sound about the stroke of noon; and you see a troop of citizens in tawdry masquerade; tabard above, heather-mixture trowser below, and the men themselves trudging in the mud among unsympathetic bystanders . . . And yet these are the heralds and Pursuivants of Scotland, who are about to proclaim a new law of the United Kingdom before two score boys, and thieves, and hackney-coachmen.'

Or this:

'Few places, if any, offer a more barbaric display of contrasts to the eye. In the very midst, one of the most satisfactory crags in nature — a Bass Rock upon dry land . . . ..'

Yes, that's better. Temples, a curiosity, sparks among smouldering volcanoes, trumpets and heralds and pursuivants and thieves, barbaric displays . . . surely eccentricity can find a toehold in all that? For the words are Robert Louis Stevenson's, from a book called *Picturesque Old Edinburgh*. The very title is another nail in the coffin of the myth, and no-one knew Edinburgh's many faces better than Stevenson.

The city has produced no more observant writer, and he observed it through the lenses of an idyllic childhood, disenchanted youth and the exile which ill-health and adulthood demanded. Distance only sharpened his perceptions and appreciation of the capital's eccentricities:

'And the story of the town is as eccentric as its appearance. For centuries it was a capital thatched with heather, and more than once, in the evil days of English invasion, it has gone up in flames to heaven a beacon to ships at sea. It was a jousting ground of jealous nobles, not only on the Greenside or by the King's Stables, where set tournaments were fought to the sound of trumpets and under the authority of the royal presence, but in every alley where there was room to cross swords, and in the mainstreet, where popular tumult under the Blue Blanket alternated with the brawls of outlandish clansmen and retainers. Down in the palace, John Knox reproved his queen in accents of modern democracy. In the town, in one of these little shops plastered like so many swallows' nests among the buttresses of the old Cathedral, that familiar autocrat, James VI, would gladly share a bottle of wine with George Heriot, the goldsmith . . ..'

Surely the myth of the staid old grey maiden resting on her fading laurels can be laid to rest now that we have established a pedigree of eccentricity unrivalled in the land? Knox, too, is ensnared as a spectacular eccentric whom as many citizens ranted against as toed his raucous line.

Edinburgh has paid the unjustly high price of a bad press for accommodating Knox's dire decades, for daring to build the 'draughty parallelograms' of the New Town, for the cutting edge of a Morningside accent, kippers and old pianos. Such straitened formality, though, inevitably contained another side which proffered a potent and fashionable stage for eccentric performances through all Edinburgh's eras. Nowadays the city becomes the stage for all the world's breathtaking assembly of eccentrics who spill with gusto into every nook and cranny of central Edinburgh each August in the Festival.

It is this richness of individual character set amid the city's teeming, turbulent and eccentric history which Jack Gillon has plundered in this book. In its pages you will find an eminent judge who believed that all children were born with tails; James Graham whose theories on fringe medicine attributed many illnesses to wool clothing, so he dressed in turf; Peter Williamson who adventured with American

Indians then returned to Edinburgh to set up the city's first postal service; James 'Balloon' Tytler who made the first balloon ascent in Britain; and the blacksmith who lived with his family in a fully-fitted cave-house.

Bizarre performances included the athletic meetings of the Six Foot High Club and an exhibition by Irish Giants. A night out at Madame Tussaud's and the Theatre Royal might end with a meal of Nor'Loch eel pie at John Dowie's Tavern; you would travel by sedan-chair under the suspicious eye of a contingent of the Town Guard, complete with Lochaber axes, and if it all proved to be much more than you could afford, there was always the chance of the debtors' refuge within the Holyrood Abbey Sanctuary.

Victorian enterprise ushered in an era of remarkable extravaganzas which included the Royal Patent Gymnasium which had as one of its main attractions a 'Patent Rotary Boat' on which 600 people would happily pay to propel themselves around in a circle; Edinburgh's first zoo; a primitive species of cinema in the Rotunda on the Mound; the vast Marine Gardens of Portobello.

Charles Blondin, the tight-rope superstar, turned up. So did Buffalo Bill's Wild West Exhibition and Congress of Rough Riders of the World. The turn of the century heralded the massive International Exhibitions, flamboyant displays of scientific and economic progress.

But not all our eccentricities are rooted in the history books. Witness the ill-starred Kinetic Sculpture of the early 'seventies. It was not just weird in itself; it seemed doomed from the start, when the switching on ceremony was restricted to sixty seconds by the power cuts of the 'Winter of Discontent'.

The original inspiration for this book was an illustration of that Victorian recreation ground, the Royal Patent Gymnasium, and it was that which launched Jack Gillon on his quest for other illustrations which would show the scatty and eccentric side of Edinburgh. His accompanying text offers colourful and thoughtful embellishments and explanations.

Author and publisher acknowledge assistance of the staff of the Edinburgh Room of the Central Library for providing most of the illustrations.

Myths die hard and Edinburgh's harsh press will not cease with the publication of this new celebration of the city's Jekyll and Hyde nature. Perhaps, though, in addition to intriguing and engaging Edinburgh's old friends and new, it will serve as an eloquent character witness for the defence next time the old diehard cynics and critics attempt to engage the reader in more predictable harangues.

Stevenson had a warning for them. A short and lightly scathing passage from his introduction to *Picturesque Old Edinburgh* angered some of his fellow citizens and delighted Glaswegians. In a later footnote, Stevenson soothed his fellows and added the following: 'To the Glasgow people I would say only one word, but that is of gold: I have not yet written a book about Glasgow'.

Jim Crumley, 1990

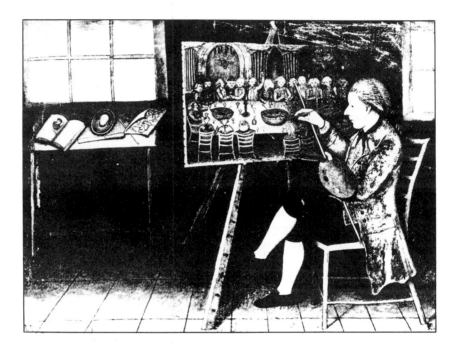

HOLYROOD ABBEY
SANCTUARY

At the foot of the Canongate, a circle of stones in the centre of the road marks the site of the Girth Cross, the boundary of the Holyrood Abbey Sanctuary, within which debtors were immune from arrest. The limits of the Abbey Sanctuary are also marked by S-shaped brass studs in the paving of the street.

The Sanctuary was established in the 12th century, under a charter granted by King David I, and was originally extended to criminals. The first record of a debtor taking sanctuary in Holyrood is in 1531.

Once over the boundary line between the Canongate and the Abbey, debtors had to make a formal application to the Bailie of Holyrood for the 'benefit and privilege' of sanctuary within twenty-four hours, or risk being ejected. After considering the case, and on payment of a booking fee, the applicant was presented with 'letters of protection' showing that he had been admitted to the Sanctuary. The debtor was then safe to live within the Sanctuary, free from the risk of arrest.

The Sanctuary's area was extensive, including Arthur's Seat and the Royal Park stretching southwards to Duddingston and Newington and eastwards to Jock's Lodge. All the habitable houses, some of which survive in the Abbey Strand, were crowded around the foot of the Canongate and accommodation for debtors was available in lodging-houses and inns.

In addition to the debtors, who were commonly known as the 'Abbey Lairds', there was a general community of tradesmen,

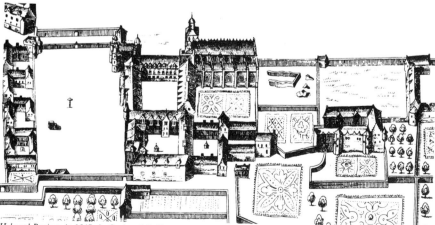

Holyrood Precincts in 1647, by Gordon of Rothiemay

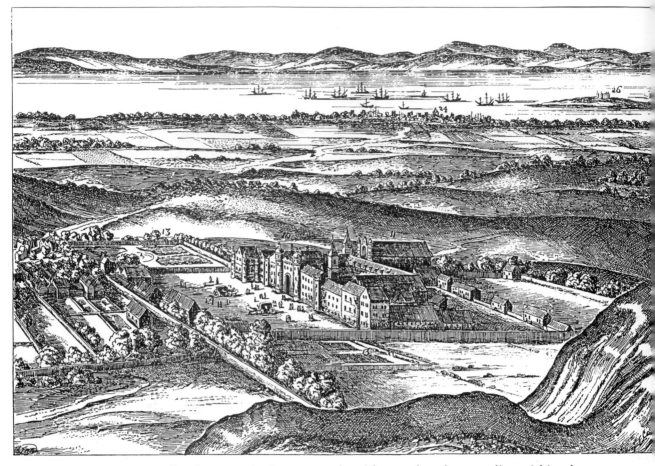

shopkeepers, innkeepers and residents who chose to live within the Sanctuary. The Bailie of Holyrood was responsible for keeping law and order within the Sanctuary, which was outside the control of the Edinburgh magistrates. This gave the Abbey Sanctuary the feeling of being a small town in its own right, independent of control from Edinburgh.

At midnight on a Saturday, the 'Abbey Lairds' could safely leave the Sanctuary for twenty-four hours of freedom as, under Scot's Law, legal proceedings could not be taken on a Sunday. Most of them took advantage of this opportunity to visit friends or go to church.

During the last 200 years of the sanctuary, Holyrood sheltered around 2,000 people. The population of debtors included clergymen, lawyers, officers of the army and navy and members of the aristocracy. Thomas De Quincey, author of *Confessions of an English Opium-eater,* was resident in the Abbey Sanctuary off and on between 1835 and 1840.

The ancient right of sanctuary within the grounds of Holyrood has never been repealed; however, the need for a debtors' sanctuary ended in 1880 when imprisonment for debt was abolished.

A REAL
TENNIS COURT

The Royal Tennis Court was in a covered building just outside the gates of Holyrood. 'Royal' or 'Real' Tennis originated in France. It is the oldest and most difficult of all ball games and was a fashionable amusement in the 16th and 17th centuries in Scotland. It is much more elaborate than modern tennis, and play involves hitting a ball with racquets both over a net and against the walls of the court. The Duke of Albany, later James VII of Scotland, was among the players in the Royal Tennis Court.

The Royal Tennis Court is also connected with early Scottish theatre. In the latter part of the 16th century, several theatre companies performed in a temporary theatre there for the amusement of the Royal Court. In 1601, an English company of actors, headed by a Laurence Fletcher, 'comedian to his Majestie', appeared at the Royal Tennis Court. Among Fletcher's company was one William Shakespeare. It is generally agreed that he visited Scotland at this time and sketched out a plan for *Macbeth*.

In 1680, players were brought to Edinburgh to entertain the nobility. Members of the Royal Family, including the future Queen Anne, took part in some of the many plays. The last recorded theatrical presentation at the Royal Tennis Court is in 1714 when *Macbeth* was performed 'in the presence of a brilliant array of Scottish Nobles, after an archery competition'.

The use of the Tennis Court as a theatre was often in defiance of the city churchmen. In 1599, the clergy took out an interdict against a company of English comedians and in 1710, the Theatre was denounced as a 'hotbed of vice and profanity'.

The Royal Tennis Court was eventually turned into a weaver's workshop and was finally burnt down in 1771. A restored Real Tennis Court at Falkland Palace is now the only one in Scotland.

INNOCENT
ART OF COCKING

Cock-fighting was introduced into Edinburgh by William Mauchrie, a teacher of fencing and cock-fighting in Edinburgh, in the first years of the 18th century. Mauchrie published an *Essay on the Innocent and Royal Recreation and Art of Cocking* in 1705, in which he noted that he had 'a special veneration and esteem for those gentlemen, about Edinburgh, who have propagated and established the Royal recreation and innocent pastime of cocking to which they have erected a cock-pit on the Links of Leith'. Admission was 10d for a ringside seat, 7d for the second row and 4d for the back row. Edinburgh Magistrates banned cock-fighting on the streets in 1704 in consequence of the 'tumults it excited and the cruel extent to which its practice had been carried'. Despite this ban, cock-fighting continued in Edinburgh well into the 19th century. Regular cock-fights or mains, as they were technically termed, were held in a cock-pit in the Grassmarket and there was a cock-pit on Leith Sands in 1804.

John Kay, the Edinburgh artist, wrote in 1785 that he found it 'surprising that noblemen and gentlemen, in the prosecution of this barbarous sport, demean themselves so far as to associate with the very lowest characters of society'.

This 'school of gambling and cruelty' was finally outlawed in the 19th century and the last cock-fight in Edinburgh was probably in 1869 when a Leith man was fined for participating.

hu... poor COCKS, exert our *Skill* & ...
... idle Gulls, and Kites that *trade* in ...

44

15

CAPTAINS OF THE CITY GUARD.

From Kays Portraits

STRANGE
GUARDIANS

The Edinburgh Town Guard was formed in 1682 to carry out the function of a local police force. The Town Guard consisted of three equally large companies, each with a lieutenant at its head. They were generally responsible for keeping order and would beat their drums through the Old Town at eight o'clock as a kind of curfew.

According to one contemporary writer, ranks were composed mainly of 'old Highlanders, of uncouth aspect and speech, dressed in a dingy red uniform with cocked hats, who often exchanged the musket for an antique native weapon called the Lochaber axe'. The 'uncouth' nature of their speech may well have been nothing more than native Gaelic, not an unreasonable preference in an 'old Highlander'. The Town Guard was not taken particularly seriously and by the time it was disbanded in 1817, it had become 'an unfailing subject of mirth to the citizens of Edinburgh'.

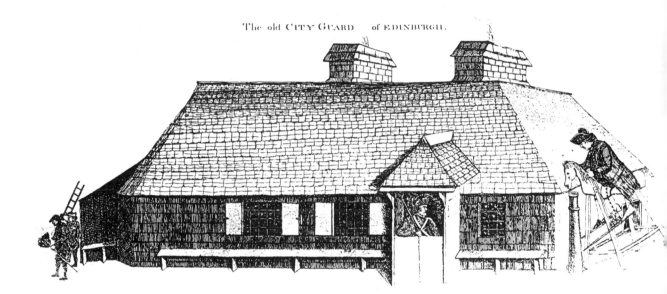

The old CITY GUARD of EDINBURGH.

The Town Guard had their base in a 'long, low, ugly' building on the north side of the High Street, opposite the Tron church. A wooden horse was kept outside the building and this was used as an unusual punishment for people found drunk and disorderly: they would be made to sit for a length of time on the horse with heavy muskets attached to their feet.

The Guard House was demolished in 1785 and the Town Guard moved to the Tolbooth.

ST ANTHONY'S
ENIGMA

The picturesque ruin of St Anthony's Chapel stands on a flat outcrop of rock, overlooking St Margaret's Loch, on the northern side of Arthur's Seat.

The Chapel was originally a simple slate-capped building with a 40-foot high tower, and appears in a view of the city as early as 1544. It remains an enigma, however, for neither the date of its construction nor its purpose is known. There is a clear view of the Chapel from Leith and the Forth, and it is possible that a light was hung in the tower to guide ships so that they might acknowledge the saint. There was almost certainly a connection between the chapel and the Knights Hospitallers of St Anthony in Leith. St Anthony was born in 250 AD and founded the first monastery in history. His relics were associated with cures for the painful skin disease, erysipelas, which was known as St Anthony's Fire. This disease was a serious problem in Edinburgh in the 15th century and a hospital was established in Leith in 1430 for its treatment. Another tradition says that the Chapel was founded for reasons connected with St Anthony's Well, a spring which rises on the slopes immediately below the Chapel.

RUINS OF ST. ANTHONY'S CHAPEL, LOOKING TOWARDS LEITH. (*From a Photograph by Alex. A. Inglis.*)

SEDENTARY
TRAVEL

The first sedan-chairs for public hire were introduced to Edinburgh in 1687. Horse-drawn coaches had been used before this, but were unsuited to the narrow closes and steep hills of the Old Town. The sedan-chair was, therefore, a particularly suitable form of transport.

The hackney-sedans were constructed of wood with a black leather covering, and were fitted with a cushioned seat. Privately-owned chairs were much more elaborate with fine embossed leather, stamped metalwork, pastoral paintings, carvings and gilding. The sedan door was normally at the front but most Edinburgh chairs had a door at the side to allow easier access from doorways in the narrow closes and wynds. Another Edinburgh adaptation was the pivoting seat which kept passengers in a horizontal position on the steep inclines in the Old Town.

The sedan-chair reached the height of its popularity in the 18th century. In 1687, there were only six chairs available for public hire but by 1779 there were 180 hackney-chairs and 50 private chairs in Edinburgh. The main sedan-chair stance was at the Tron Kirk. A table of fares introduced in 1738 specified 6d for a trip within the city, 4s for a whole day's rental, and 1s 6d for a journey a half-mile outside town. The majority of the chair-bearers were Highlanders and this was reflected in the use of tartan for their uniforms.

It was a quirky taxi service. The 'ladies of nobility and quality' who used them for trips to dancing assemblies and the theatre could be sure — doubtless at a price — of a small lantern to light the sedan and a hot-water pan placed under the seat.

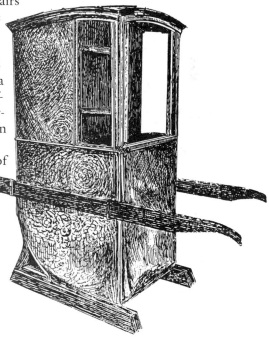

Sedan Chair from Lord Milton's House.

A particularly eccentric Edinburgh judge never used a sedan himself but had his wig sent home in one when it rained. A sedan was even kept by the Royal Infirmary as an ambulance. It was quite common for sedans to be overturned in strong winds and it was normal on windy days to hire two men to walk either side of the chair to keep it even, while another two carried it. Quite how four such men synchronised their movements is not explained.

The sedan-chair continued to be used for all major Edinburgh social events well into the 19th century, but by that time most sedans were in the more affluent New Town. There were 101 sedan-chairs in 1814, only 46 in 1827 and, by 1850, this picturesque method of transport had been replaced by horse-drawn carriages. Now, in the 1990s, they are back in the Old Town as a tourist attraction.

THE LORD HIGH COMMISSIONER'S CHAIR

BUITH-RAW
AND KRAMES

The earliest method of selling merchandise in Medieval Edinburgh was from stalls in one of the city's market places. Artisans and craftsmen soon started to require a more permanent base for their specialised workshops, and in 1440 a number of timber fronted two-storey buildings, called the 'buith-raw', were erected on the High Street to the north of St Giles. Over the years, the buith-raw was extended and heightened until it consisted of seven tenement buildings stretching the full length of St Giles. They were renamed the 'Luckenbooths', from the fact that the buildings contained lockable booths.

The Luckenbooths were linked at their west end to the Bell-house, the meeting place of the Edinburgh guilds, and the Tolbooth, Sir Walter Scott's Heart of Midlothian. The site of the Tolbooth is still

marked by blocks in the street. The Luckenbooths were the focus of trade and business for centuries. The shops dealt in a wide range of goods and services. These included Peter Williamson's Penny Post Office and Alan Ramsay's circulating library, from which he 'diffused plays and other works of fiction among the people of Edinburgh'. Ramsay's shop at the eastmost end of the Luckenbooths was later used by William Creech as a bookshop which became the 'natural resort of lawyers, authors, and all sorts of literary idlers who were always buzzing about this convenient hive'. Creech was responsible for the publication of early work by Burns.

In the narrow passage left between the Luckenbooths and St Giles were shops or stalls called Krames or Creams. The Krames were 'singular places of business, often not presenting more space than a good church-pew' and the stalls specialised in hardware, leather goods and toys. Various Orders of the Town Council attempted to stop residents of the flats above the Luckenbooths throwing household refuse out of their back windows on to the Krames, but they were unpersuasive, and the close through the Luckenbooths to the Krames was known as the Stinking Style.

The Luckenbooths were finally demolished in 1817, by which time the High Street — now only 15 feet wide — had become hopelessly congested.

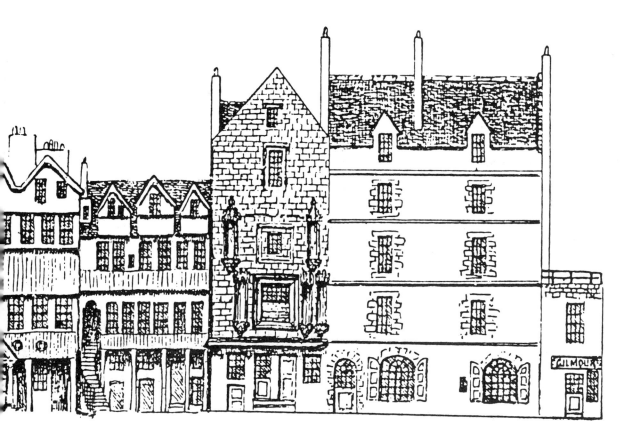

JOHN KAY

No-one has captured the eccentric nature of Edinburgh more tellingly than John Kay, a miniaturist artist and painter for around forty years until his death in 1826. He produced around nine hundred etchings which represent a unique record of the events and people of Edinburgh.

Kay could have made a lucrative living from commissioned portraits, but he was drawn to the curious, eccentric and humorous aspects of Edinburgh life and given to producing 'freaks of his fancy'.

JOHN KAY
Drawn & Engraved by Himself 1786.

These were often satirical caricatures, which on at least one occasion resulted in his being 'cudgelled', and in 1792 he successfully defended himself against a prosecution brought by an individual who was offended by one of his etchings.

His portraits are described as 'the most exact and faithful likeness that could have been produced by any mode of art. He drew the man as he walked the street every day; his gait, his costume, every peculiarity of his appearance, done to a point'. Kay's rare talent has left a vivid account of life in Edinburgh around the turn of the 19th century.

ODDBALL
MONBODDO

Lord Monboddo was one of the most respected and eminent Judges at the Court of Session during the 18th century, but he was also something of an oddball. He had a passionate attachment to the ways of the Ancient Greeks and a contempt for anything he considered to be modern. As a result he lived very simply. If the Ancient Greeks didn't use it, neither did he. He travelled only on horseback, for example, as coaches and sedan-chairs were new inventions.

He refused to sit on the Bench with his fellow judges but sat underneath with the court clerks. This was due to a decision which went against him when he was the claimant in a case involving the value of a horse.

In 1773, he published a notorious book *Of the Origin and Progress of Language*. It included the theories that man was derived from animals, that orang-utangs were related to humans and capable of speech, and that in the Bay of Bengal there was a nation of human creatures with tails. These ideas 'afforded endless matter for jest by the wags of the day', but today are seen to be related to the theory of evolution. Slightly more eccentric was his belief that babies are born with tails and that midwives cut them off at birth.

In 1785, when he was 71, Lord Monboddo was visiting the King's Court in London when part of the ceiling of the courtroom started to collapse. There was a great rush from the building, until the danger was past and order restored. Lord Monboddo, who was deaf and short-sighted, was the only person who did not move from his seat. When asked why, he explained that he thought it was 'an annual ceremony, with which, as an alien, he had nothing to do'.

O.W.L.'S
SERVANT

Eighteenth century Edinburgh was a popular venue for itinerant medical shows. A stage would be erected on the High Street and dancers, jugglers, acrobats and rope-dancers (who performed on a tight-rope fixed between buildings on either side of the High Street) would attract a crowd. The Medicine Man of the company would then detail the curative powers of the pills, powders and potions he had to sell — 'infallible' antidotes for almost all disorders. Edinburgh folk were gullible enough to keep them in business.

One of the most notorious of these medical quacks was 'Doctor' James Graham, who was born in the Grassmarket in 1745. In 1780, he established the lavish 'Temple of Health' in Royal Terrace, London. Here he treated patients with his imposing and elaborate electrical machines with such lethal-sounding names as the 'magnetic throne' and the 'electric bath tub'. Concoctions like his 'famous aetherial and balsamic medicines' and 'elixir of life' contained ingredients which he claimed

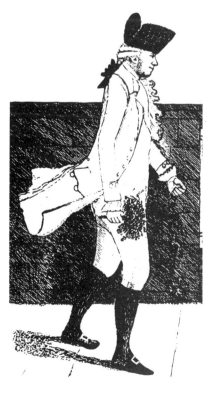

prolonged life indefinitely. Clients could also sample the richly gilded 'celestial bed', filled with stallion hair and guaranteed to cure sterility, and his 'earth bath', which promised beneficial results from being buried up to the chin in warm earth. What it benefited is not related. The 'Temple of Health' was popular at first, but soon fell out of favour and closed in 1782.

In 1783, he returned to Edinburgh where he lectured, treated patients with his electrical equipment, sold patent medicines and copies of his book, *The Guardian of Health, Happiness and Long Life*. But after his lecture, 'On the means of exciting and rendering permanent the Rational, Temperate and Serene Pleasures of the married state', he was banned from addressing the public due to the 'coarseness and indecency' of its content.

He believed that man should 'abstain totally from flesh and blood, from all liquors but cold water and fresh milk, and from 'excessive sensual indulgence', and that many human ailments were due to wearing woollen clothing. The Edinburgh artist, John Kay, depicts him in

his usual white linen clothes. He considered fresh air important to health and applied to build a house at the top of Arthur's Seat, 'to experience the utmost degree of cold that the climate in Edinburgh had to offer'. Mercifully, his application was turned down, doubtless for the good of Arthur's Seat's health.

Graham gradually became more and more eccentric. He gave public demonstrations of his 'earth bath', decided he was a messenger from heaven and called himself 'The Servant of the Lord, O.W.L.' (Oh! Wonderful Love!), and in 1792, he fasted for fifteen days and wore cut-turfs for clothing. Eventually he had to be put under restraint in his own house.

For all his obsessions with health, he died suddenly from a ruptured blood vessel in a house in Buccleuch Street, in 1794, at the age of 49.

INDIAN PETER

Peter Williamson, or 'Indian Peter' as he became known, was one of the more colourful personalities of 18th century Scotland. He had a quite remarkable life.

Peter was born in 1730, the son of a crofter, at Hirnlay in the Parish of Aboyne, Aberdeenshire. His parents were 'reputable, though not rich' and they sent him, as a young boy, to live with an aunt in Aberdeen.

At this time, the kidnapping business was flourishing in Aberdeen. Children were regularly kidnapped for sale in American plantations and a number of the Aberdeen Bailies, who were in partnership with the kidnappers, amassed fortunes from this 'hideous traffic in human merchandise'. The trade was at its briskest between 1740 and 1746 when more than 600 children from the Aberdeen area were transported to America.

In January, 1743, at the age of 13, Peter was playing on the harbour at Aberdeen when he was 'taken notice of by two fellows employed by some worthy merchants of the town, in that villainous practice called kidnapping'. He was 'marked out by these monsters as their prey and taken forcibly on board a ship'. Peter was shipped across the Atlantic and sold as a slave in Philadelphia for the 'handsome sum' of £16.

Peter was indentured for a period of seven years to a fairly well-off planter, Hugh Wilson, who had himself been kidnapped as a boy. Peter describes Wilson as a 'humane, honest and worthy man', and, contrary to the normal harsh conditions of slavery in America, he treated Peter kindly. Just as Peter's period of indenture was about to end, Hugh Wilson died and bequeathed Peter '£120, his best horse, saddle and all his wearing apparel'.

At 24, he married the daughter of a wealthy planter. His father-in-law provided a dowry of 200 acres of land on the frontiers of the province of Pennsylvania and Peter settled down to the life of a farmer. But neighbouring Red Indians began to prove troublesome, instigated by the French who paid £15 for every British scalp taken.

On the night of October 2, 1754, Peter was in his house alone when it was surrounded by Cherokee Indians. He was captured, his house plundered and burned. He was used as a pack-horse by the Indians and force marched many miles, witnessing along the way the murder and scalping of numerous settlers. Peter survived, however, and made a daring escape, but when he finally arrived at his father-in-law's home, he learned that his wife had died two months before.

He was called before the State Assembly in Philadelphia to pass on any information he had acquired during his captivity and enlisted in one of the army regiments set up to combat the French and the Indians. He remained in the army for two years, rising to the rank of Lieutenant, but he was finally taken prisoner by the French, marched to Quebec, and there embarked as an exchange prisoner on a ship bound for Plymouth, where he arrived in November 1756. Some months later, Peter was discharged as being unfit for further service, due to a wound in his left hand. With only a small gratuity of six shillings, he set off to walk to his hometown of Aberdeen.

He arrived penniless in York, where he was fortunate enough to interest 'certain honourable and influential men' in his case. They assisted him in the publication of an account of his unusual adventures and experiences. The book was catchily titled French and Indian Cruelty, exemplified in the *Life and various Vicissitudes of Fortune of Peter Williamson, who was carried off from Aberdeen in his Infancy, and sold as a slave in Pennsylvania*. It gave remarkably good value for money, made excellent reading and created quite a stir in York. A thousand copies were sold and Peter made a net profit of £30 with which to continue his journey to Scotland.

He made some additional money on his travels northwards by selling copies of his book and giving displays of Indian life: 'Armed to the teeth and painted like a Red Indian, he would enter a town, whooping and screeching until he had attracted a sufficiently large crowd. Then he would windmill his arms madly and give his impression of a war-dance.' At the end of the show, he would take up a collection and sell copies of his book. Today, the Wogan show fulfils much the same role.

In June, 1758, Peter finally arrived in Aberdeen, where his exhibition of American Indian culture attracted great crowds and his book sold well. The details of his kidnapping horrified the Aberdeen public. The merchants and Magistrates of Aberdeen also took note of the book, particularly the part which accused them of being involved in the kidnapping business, and Peter was charged with offering for sale a 'scurrilous and infamous libel upon the merchants and magistrates of the town'. His case was heard by the magistrates' own tribunal, so it was not difficult to secure a conviction: the magistrates were the aggrieved party as well as the judges. Copies of the book were seized and burned at the market-cross by the common-hangman. Peter was forced to sign a declaration that the account of his kidnapping was false and was fined five shillings. He was finally banished from Aberdeen as a vagrant.

It was then that he made for Edinburgh, and found the city and its people much to his liking. The large hall in which the Scottish Parliament had met was then a central meeting place associated with the adjoining law courts, and here Peter established a coffee-house which became a

favourite howff of lawyers and their clients. The coffee-house consisted of 'three or four very small apartments, one within another; the partitions made of the thinnest materials; some of them even of brown paper'.

Robert Fergusson's poem, *The Rising of the Session*, describes the lawyers departing for their summer break and devotes a verse to Peter's coffee-house:

This vacance is a heavy doom
On Indian Peter's coffee-room,
For a' his china pigs are toom
Nor do we see
In wine the sucker bisket soom
As light's a flee.*

Peter sold copies of his book in the coffee-house and he was encouraged by his lawyer customers to raise an action against the magistrates of Aberdeen. The case was heard in the Court of Session and the verdict was unanimous in Peter's favour. The Provost of Aberdeen, four bailies and the Dean of Guild were ordered to pay a fine of £100 sterling, as compensation to Peter.

Peter then proceeded to raise an action for damages against 'Bailie William Fordyce and others' who had been personally responsible for his kidnapping. It was agreed that the matter should be decided by arbitration and the Sheriff-Substitute of Aberdeenshire, James Forbes, was appointed arbiter. James Forbes was best known for his convivial habits and, when he delayed his decision on the case until only 48 hours before the matter would return automatically to the jurisdiction of the Court of Session, both sides decided to speed up the process.

The Sheriff-Substitute was bribed with vast amounts of food and drink at various taverns in the City over the following two days. He finally gave a verdict in favour of the kidnappers, after which he retired to bed 'very merry and jocose' and slept all the next day 'dead drunk and speechless'. The decree, which exonerated Bailie Fordyce and his fellow kidnappers, was hurriedly drawn up and read aloud the following morning at the market-cross.

The circumstances of the decision were brought to the attention of the Court of Session and Peter was able to produce evidence of the involvement of the bailie and his companions in his kidnapping. The court reversed the earlier decision and in December, 1763, Peter was

*vacance, vacation; pigs, bottles; toom, empty; sucker bisket, sugar biscuit; soom, swim

awarded £200 damages with 100 guineas legal costs.

During these legal actions, Peter had also been busy in other areas. He had a lively and ingenious mind, and 'aided by the knowledge he had acquired in scenes more bustling than the Scottish Capital, he became a projector of schemes, locally new and unheard of, some of course visionary, but others practicable and likely to be generally useful'.

He became the proprietor of a famous tavern in Edinburgh's Old Parliament Close and, as a result of his earlier adventures, the sign over the tavern read: PETER WILLIAMSON, VINTNER FROM THE OTHER WORLD. Peter is described as being a 'robust, stout, athletic man and a great wag, of very jocular manners' and must have been a popular landlord. His occasional exhibitions, when he dressed as a Delaware Indian, were an attraction of considerable interest. A wooden figure of him in Indian dress used to stand as a signpost outside the tavern. The Edinburgh magistrates assembled at Peter's tavern for the 'deid chack', the dinner they took after attending a hanging.

In 1773, Peter compiled Edinburgh's first street directory. This pioneering work contained an 'alphabetical list of the names and places of abode of the Members of the College of Justice, public and private gentlemen, merchants, and other eminent traders; mechanics, carriers, and all persons in public business. Where at one view, you have a plain direction, pointing out the streets, wynds, closes, lands, and other places of their residence in and about the metropolis'. The directory cost one shilling and Peter continued to publish it until 1796.

The directory was a product of his new business venture, a printing-house in the Luckenbooths. In 1769, he had brought a new portable printing press from London and taught himself the craft of printing. He also invented a portable printing press which was able to print two folio pages, 'with the greatest expedition and exactness', and he would travel with his press to country fairs giving 'exhibitions of the wonder of printing to the astonished rustics'. At the same time, he developed stamps and ink for marking linen and books 'which stands washing, boiling and bleaching, and is more regular and beautiful than any needle'.

In 1776, he launched a weekly periodical, *The Scots Spy* or *Critical Observer*, which ran for a total of ten

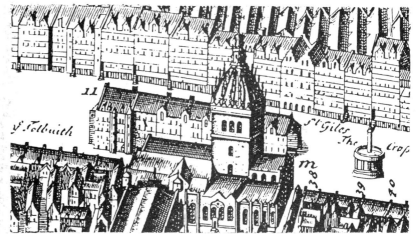

months. It was published every Friday and consisted of a hotch-potch of local gossip and articles.

During the time that Peter ran the coffee-house, he was frequently asked to arrange the delivery of letters and he employed a man to deliver them for a small charge. This gave Peter the idea for one of his most successful ventures - a regular postal service throughout the city.

The earliest information about this is an advertisement in the second edition of his *Edinburgh Directory* published in 1774: 'The Publisher takes this opportunity to acquaint the Public that he will always make it his study to dispatch all letters and parcels, not exceeding three pounds in weight, to any place within an English mile to the east, south and west of the cross of Edinburgh, and as far as South and North Leith, every hour through the day for one penny each letter and bundle.'

The main office for Peter's postal service was in the Luckenbooths and he appointed seventeen shopkeepers in different parts of the city as official receivers of letters. He employed four uniformed postmen, who wore on their hats the words Penny Post and were numbered 1, 4, 8 and 16, so that the business seemed much larger. Peter's Penny Post was the first in Britain and he ran it for thirty years. In 1793, Peter's Penny Post was integrated into the General Post Office and he received a pension of £25 for the goodwill of the business.

In Robert Fergusson's poem, *Codicile to Robert Fergusson's Last Will*, he mentions Peter's Penny Post:

To Williamson, and his resetters
Dispersing of the burial letters,
That they may pass with little cost
Fleet on the wings of penny-post.

In his later days, Peter returned to his old business and kept a tavern at Gavinloch's Land in the Lawnmarket, where it is thought that he ultimately became 'addicted to drink'.

He died on January 19, 1799 and was buried in an unmarked grave in the Old Calton Cemetery, about fifteen paces north-east of the Martyr's Monument. The *Scot's Magazine* wrote:

'At Edinburgh, Mr. Peter Williamson, well known for his various adventures through life. He was kidnapped when a boy at Aberdeen, and sent to America, for which he afterwards recovered damages. He passed a considerable time among the Cherokees, and on his return to Edinburgh amused the public with a description of their manners and customs, and his adventures among them, assuming the dress of one of their chiefs, imitating the war whoop, &c. He had the merit of first instituting a Penny-post in Edinburgh, for which, when it was assumed by Government, he received a pension. He also was the first who published a Directory, so essentially useful in a large city.'

CARTOON
CHARACTER

'Bailie' Jamie Duff was a bailie in nobody's mind but his own, but 18th century Edinburgh so enjoyed his antics that he derived an income from public donations. He was of 'weak intellect, and odd but harmless manners; tall and robust with a shambling gait and was unable to speak clearly, except when irritated when his swearing was quite distinct'.

Jamie achieved early fame when he entered himself in the horse-races at Leith. He ran the course in bare feet, bent over, and whipping himself, in farcical parody of horse and rider. Presumably the odds were fairly long. Next he developed an ambition to be a magistrate and would walk around the town wearing a brass chain, cocked hat and wig. He was such a popular character that his impression of a bailie was met with cheerful good humour by most people. A real bailie took offence, however, at what he considered to be a mockery of his position, and Jamie's brass chain of office was confiscated. This petty abuse of power was satirised in verse and cartoons.

Jamie also had a passion for attending funerals and went to almost every funeral in Edinburgh for around forty years. It became that no funeral in Edinburgh was considered complete without 'Bailie' Jamie Duff leading the procession. He always dressed in his well-worn mourning costume of black cravat and hat which he dyed deeper black for special funerals. It became customary to pay a shilling or half a crown for Jamie's services.

Such was his confused sense of logic, however, that he developed an aversion to silver money, as the Army was bribing people to enlist with silver coins. As a result, he refused nearly all offers of money — a disastrous course of action for one whose income consisted mainly of donations from the Edinburgh public. Jamie's mother spared his blushes by appointing his nephew, who was too young to be enlisted, to act as purse-bearer and accept money on his behalf.

Jamie lived with his mother, who was a poor widow, in the Cowgate. He was very fond of her and when he was asked out by friends to share a meal, Jamie would put his portions of food in his pocket to take back to his mother. The fact that he made no distinction between solid and liquid food and pocketed both together does not detract from the thoughtfulness of the gesture, however messy the consequences.

THEATRE·BY·GASLIGHT

Edinburgh's long conflict between church and theatre more or less abated with the opening of the Theatre Royal in 1769 in Shakespeare Square, now the site of the Post Office in Waterloo Place.

Shortly before the opening, one observer wrote that church ministers had been 'zealous for the good of their flock and had preached against theatrical performances, however, the players have once more taken the field, and the clergy leave them to their ungodliness'.

The following description of the Theatre Royal is from an account

THEATRE ROYAL, EDINBURGH.

by the English writer Edward Topham who visited Edinburgh in 1775:

'The Theatre is situated at the end of the New Bridge in the New Town, and on the outside is a plain structure like most others of the same nature. It is of an oblong form, and designed after the manner of foreign ones. I do not know its exact dimensions; but at three shillings (which is the price of admittance into the pit and boxes) it is capable of containing about one hundred and thirty pounds. The ornaments are few and in an unaffected plain style, which, on the whole, has a very elegant appearance. It is lighted with gas, and the scenery is well painted. The upper galleries, or, as they obligingly term them, 'the Gods', seem here very compassionate Divinities. You sometimes hear the murmurings of displeasure at a distance; but they never rain down oranges, apples, &c., on the heads of the unfortunate actors. They suffer them very quietly to 'strut their hour upon the stage,' and show their dislike by not applauding them.'

Sarah Siddons, the leading tragic actress of her time, appeared at the Theatre Royal in May, 1784. Demand for tickets for her performances was tremendous. People queued all night and the army had to be called in to control the over-enthusiastic crowds.

The Theatre Royal existed until 1859, when it was demolished to make way for the Post Office. The Queen's Theatre in Broughton Street was then re-named the Theatre Royal, until it was destroyed by fire in 1946.

APPLE GLORY

Sarah Sibbald, or 'Apple Glory' as she was known, was a character who was long associated with the Theatre Royal. She was a street trader, who had a fruit-barrow at the corner of the Theatre Royal building.

She is described as being 'stout — very stout — with a bright kindly face as rosy as the finest of her best apples and a character as good as her fruit'. So esteemed was she that when the work for the erection of the Post Office got under way, she was installed on a raised platform, where with shelter from the weather, she carried on her business 'in great style'.

JOHN DOWIE'S
TAVERN

The teeming nature of life in 18th century Edinburgh elevated the Old Town's taverns to a critical role in the city's social life. 'Intemperance was the rule and no man of the day thought himself able to dispense with the Meridian' (the drink taken at midday). Much of the business life of the city was carried out in taverns — some things never change — and it was even normal for doctors to consult their patients there.

One of the most popular establishments was John Dowie's Tavern in Libberton's Wynd, a narrow lane sloping down to the Cowgate, just to the east of the junction of the present day High Street and George IV Bridge. This 'perfect specimen of tavern' was run by 'Dainty' John Dowie. The most eminent citizens, including David Hume and Burns, frequented Dowie's 'quaint house of entertainment for its congenial company and good fare'.

The following description was typical of the taverns of the day: 'a great portion of this house was without light, consisting of a series of windowless chambers, decreasing in size till the smallest was a mere box, of irregular oblong shape, designated the Coffin'. The largest room could accommodate fourteen people, the Coffin held four, at a squeeze, and only two of the rooms had windows.

The Tavern was renowned for its Archibald Younger's Edinburgh Ale, 'a potent fluid which almost glued the lips of the drinker together and of which few could despatch more than a bottle' — though many tried — and was also famed for its 'petit soupers', the speciality of the house being Nor' Loch eel-pie.

John Dowie was the 'sleekest and kindest of all landlords' and 'conscientious as to money matters'. He left a fortune — £6,000 — when he died in 1817. The new owner of the Tavern displayed on his signboard the name 'Burns' Tavern late Johnnie Dowie', capitalising on the fame of the previous landlord and the link with Burns.

JOHNNIE DOWIE'S ALE

A' ye wha wis', on e'enings lang,
To meet an' crack, and sing a sang,
And weet your pipes, for little wrang,
To purse or person,
To sere Johnnie Dowie's gang,
There thrum a verse on.

O, Dowie's ale! thou art the thing,
That gars us crack, and gars us sing,
Cast by our cares, our wants a' fling
Frae us wi' anger;
Thou e'en mak'st passion tak the wing,
Or thou wilt bang 'er.

How blest is he wha has a groat
To spare upon the cheering pot;
He may look blithe as ony Scot
That e'er was born:
Gie's a' the like, but wi' a coat,
And guide frae scorn.

But thinkna that strong ale alone
Is a' that's kept by dainty John;
Na, na; for in the place there's none,
Frae end to end,
For meat can set you better on,
Than can your friend.

Wi' looks as mild as mild can be,
An' smudgin' laugh, wi' winkin' e'e;
An' lowly bow down to his knee,
He'll say fu' douce,
'Whe, gentlemen, stay till I see,
What's i' the house.'

Anither bow- 'Deed, gif ye please,
Ye can get a bit toasted cheese,
A crum o' tripe, ham, dish o' pease,
(The season fittin',)
An egg, or, cauler frae from the seas,
A fleuk or whitin';

A nice beefsteak, or ye may get
A gude buff'd herring, reisted skate,
An' ingans, an'(tho' past its date),
A cut o' veal;
Ha, ha, it's no that unco late,
I'll do it weel.'

Then, pray for's health this mony year,
Fresh three-'n-a-ha'penny, best o' beer,
That can (tho' dull) you brawly cheer-
Recant you weel up;
An' gar you a' forget your wear-
Your sorrows seal up.

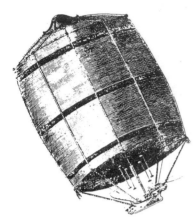

GRAND EDINBURGH
FIRE
BALLOON

James Balloon Tytler was a spectacular Jack-of-all-trades — surgeon, writer, publisher, composer, and poet — but his claim to fame is rooted firmly in the day he made aviation history. The 'Grand Edinburgh Fire Balloon', which he invented, created a great deal of excitement in 1784 and ultimately resulted in Britain's first manned aerial ascent.

Tytler was an eccentric and luckless character, described by Burns as an 'obscure, tippling though extraordinary body', and both his epic flight and his other great achievement — the eight years he spent compiling the 10-volume second edition of the *Encyclopaedia Britannica* — are both largely overlooked.

He worked as a surgeon and an apothecary, wrote numerous books and articles, published periodicals and a newspaper, invented a printing machine and a process for bleaching linen, and composed songs, poems and tunes for the bagpipes. None of these activities made much money — he was paid a pittance of 16/- a week for writing the *Encyclopaedia* — although a number of them made money for others, and he was outlawed as a debtor at least twice.

The successful flights of the Montgolfier brothers in France, in 1783, fired Tytler with enthusiasm for ballooning and in June, 1784, he exhibited the 'Grand Edinburgh Fire Balloon' in the uncompleted dome of Robert Adam's Register House. The 'Fire Balloon' was barrel-shaped, 40 feet high and 30 feet in diameter, and powered by heating the air in the balloon with a stove. Weather conditions prevented the first attempt at a flight early in August but, on August 27, in Comely Gardens, an open area north-east of Holyrood, Tytler tried again. Wearing only a cork jacket for protection, he seated himself in a small wicker packing case tied to the base of the balloon. When the ropes holding the balloon were released, it soared to 350 feet, travelled half a mile, and landed in Restalrig village. Tytler found the flight 'most agreeable with no giddiness' and he 'amused himself by looking at the spectators below'.

This first flight was made in front of a small number of people early in the morning, but news of his success ensured that the next appearance

of the 'Fire Balloon' four days later was a major public event. A large paying audience gathered in the Comely Gardens, and the slopes of Arthur's Seat and Calton Hill were also crowded with people eager to witness this historic occasion. At 2 pm, the balloon was inflated for half an hour and, with Tytler again in the basket, rose to 100 feet, sailed over the pavilion and descended gradually on the other side. This 'leap' was not particularly remarkable but the spectators were delighted. All subsequent exhibitions of the 'Grand Edinburgh Fire Balloon' were disasters. One newspaper considered that enough time had been 'trifled away on this misshapen smoke-bag' and in the excitement of the flamboyant Vincent Lunardi's very successful balloon ascent from Edinburgh, in October, 1785, the unfortunate James 'Balloon' Tytler was forgotten.

In 1792, Tytler fled Edinburgh for Ireland, after being arrested for producing anti-government pamphlets, and three years later he emigrated to Salem, Massachusetts. There, on a stormy night in January, 1804, the Scottish aviation pioneer drowned whilst walking home.

IRISH GIANTS
ON PARADE

One of the most unlikely show-stoppers in any roll-call of eccentric Edinburgh was an exhibition of Irish Giants in the 1780s.

Charles Byrne, in the centre of the illustration, was eight feet two inches tall and travelled the country 'exhibiting his huge person to the public', which is the sort of publicity you could get away with then. While in Edinburgh, he had to crawl on all fours to get up and down the narrow stairs in the Old Town and alarmed people by lighting his pipe at street lamps, 'which he did with the greatest of ease, without standing even on tiptoe'.

The other two 'wonderful and surprising Gigantic Twin Brothers' in the illustration were also Irish and visited Edinburgh in July 1784. They appeared in a ladies' hairdresser's in Princes Street, admittance one shilling. These 'extraordinary young men' were both eight feet tall and 'truly shaped and proportioned to their height'. The sight of them is described as being 'more than the mind can conceive, the tongue express, or pencil delineate'. Big attractions don't come much bigger.

The twins left Edinburgh after a few months, with the intention of visiting other towns to 'astonish the natives'.

LITTLE &
LARGE

Patrick Cotter O'Brien, 'The Wonder of the Age' appeared in Edinburgh in February 1803. He was eight feet one inch, weighed five hundredweight (eight stones, one hundredweight, remember?) He was born in Ireland in 1760 and 'travelled the country for many years, exhibiting himself to all those who chose to gratify their curiousity at a trifling expense'. . . by which he meant that he simply turned up.

While he was in Edinburgh, O'Brien decided to be fitted for a greatcoat by Deacon Jollie, whose tailor's shop was on Old Assembly Close. This 'trifling incident' created quite a stir. People came from all parts of the city to see what was undoubtedly the largest coat ever made in Edinburgh. The public were also curious to discover how a man as small as Deacon Jollie had accomplished the task of measuring the giant O'Brien. Deacon Jollie maintained a 'solemn silence' on the subject and the caricature, published at the time, provides a possible answer.

SIX FOOT HIGH CLUB

The Six Foot High Club was established in Edinburgh in 1826 and membership was restricted to people of six feet or more. The club activities centred around athletics and gymnastics at a gymnasium in East Thistle Street and a training ground in Malta Terrace.

The dress uniform of the Club was 'the finest dark green cloth coat, double breasted with special buttons and a velvet collar. On special occasions, a tile hat was worn'.

The Club also seems to have had a literary interest. Exceptions to the six foot rule were made to grant honorary membership to Sir Walter Scott, who was the Club Umpire, and James Hogg, who was the club's poet laureate.

LEITH RACES

For almost 200 years — from 1620 to 1816 — the main venue for horse-racing in Scotland was a long stretch of beach east of Leith harbour, on the site now occupied by the docks.

The Leith Races week was normally at the end of July or the beginning of August, and was the sporting event of the year in Scotland. The races attracted great crowds of people from all over the country, and kept the city in a 'state of feverish excitation and caused a general suspension of work and business'.

As the race week was run by the town council, a uniformed city officer marched to the Races every morning, 'bearing aloft at the end of a long pole the gaily-ornamented city purse'. The racegoers walked with him down Leith Walk so that he 'disappeared amidst the moving myriads, until only the purse at the end of the pole revealed his presence'.

Great care was taken to have the sands measured off and in good

order for the horses, and proclamations were issued prohibiting digging for bait, for example, until the Races were over.

Prizes included the City of Edinburgh purse of £50, His Majesty's purse of 100 guineas and the Ladies Subscription of 50 guineas. On the last day of the meeting, there was a purse for the horses beaten in the earlier part of the week.

The racing seems to have been subsidiary to other activities on the sands. These included shows, wheels of fortune and refreshment at the 'vast lines of drinking booths which stretched along the shore'. For an entire week, the town was 'one continued scene of racing, drinking and fighting'.

The race meeting was usually concluded by the 'general demolition of the stalls and booths and a fighting match amongst those that were able to keep their legs, a riotous brawl being maintained by the returning crowds along the entire length of Leith Walk'.

In 1816, the horse-racing was transferred to Musselburgh Links, as the smooth turf provided an improved track. Attempts were later made to re-establish the Leith Races, but the Council refused permission due to the increasing pressure of public opinion against the 'drunkenness and excesses' associated with the event.

PORTOBELLO-ON-SEA

Portobello originated in the mid-18th century when a retired sailor, George Hamilton, built a cottage named Puerto Bella on what was 'a desolate spot frequented by robbers and smugglers'.

Portobello soon became a popular seaside location and was 'greatly resorted to during the summer months by the Edinburgh upper classes'. Its distance from Edinburgh and the lack of public transport restricted visitors to those who had use of a private carriage or an expensive seaside residence.

Seaside attractions at Portobello included a mile-long sandy beach, clear sea water, pure air and two mineral springs. The power station came later. In June, 1795, a newspaper advertisement announced that

'Bathing-machines upon the best construction, with sturdy horses and careful drivers' were available for hire at Portobello. The Bathing-machines were dressing-rooms on wheels which were drawn into the sea by horses. In 1806, Portobello Hot & Cold Sea-Water Baths were opened and soon became very fashionable. There was no promenade then and, during the summer, the beach was frequently lined with carriages belonging to the 'fashion and rank of Edinburgh'.

One of the town's strangest buildings — Portobello Tower — was erected in 1785 as a summer house and restored in 1864 as part of a large house. The Tower is octagonal, originally four storeys high and built in stone from demolished buildings in Edinburgh's Old Town. It can still be seen at the west end of the Promenade. In 1806, a stagecoach service between Edinburgh and Portobello was introduced and larger crowds followed. Punch and Judy shows, gingerbread sellers, horse racing, itinerant entertainers and circus performances entertained the crowds through its 19th century hey-day.

THE TOWER.

BRUNTSFIELD LINKS

Bruntsfield Links was originally the Burgh Muir, Edinburgh's common grazing ground and the area to which victims of the plague were banished in 1645.

Later, two of the world's pioneering golf clubs were established on the Links (a fitting enough adaptation — a species of plague still inflicts many a golfer). These were the Burghers or Burgess Golfing Society, founded in 1735, and the Honourable Company of Edinburgh Golfers (1744). Golf was so popular in Edinburgh at this time that the town council instituted a trophy, a silver club, as an annual prize for members of the Honourable Company.

'COCK O'THE GREEN'

Alexander McKellar was one of Bruntsfield's most famous players or 'Cock o' the Green'. He was a player of great skill and dedication and would spend the whole day on Bruntsfield Links, often playing at night by the light of a hand lantern.

DAFT WILLIE GUNN

In the early 19th century 'Daft' Willie Gunn was a well known caddie on the Bruntsfield Links. His notoriety and reputation for daftness seems to have resulted from his habit of wearing numerous layers of coats, hats, shirts and trousers all at the same time.

GILMERTON TROGLODYTES

A narrow door on the west side of Drum Street in Gilmerton, Edinburgh is the entrance to 'the subterranean chambers of a remarkable cave'. The following account was given by the Rev Thomas Whyte, parish minister of Liberton, in 1792:

'Here is a famous cave dug out of rock by one George Paterson, a smith. It was finished in 1724 after five years hard labour as appears from the inscription on one of the chimney-heads. In this cave are several apartments, several beds, a spacious table with a large punch-bowl all cut out of the rock in the nicest manner. Here there was a forge with a well and washing-house. Here there were several windows which communicated light from above. The author of this extraordinary piece of workmanship after he had finished it, lived in it for a long time with his wife and family and prosecuted his business as a smith. He died in it about the year 1735. He was a feuar of feodary and consequently the cave he formed and embellished so much and the garden above it was his own property, and his posterity enjoyed it for some time after his decease. His cave for many years was deemed as a great curiosity and visited by all the people of fashion.'

Whyte's account stuck, and it was a hundred years before it was challenged. Meanwhile, there were reports of holiday parties coming from Edinburgh to view his 'singular house' and judges 'imbibing liquor in his stone parlour'. It seems he was also 'forgiven the yearly duty and public burdens, on account of the extraordinary labour he had incurred in making himself a home'.

The cave is about ten feet below the surface and is reached by a flight of twelve steps which lead into a 40-feet long passage with an unusual series of rooms and passages on each side. Immediately to the right at the foot of the stairs is a recess like a blacksmith's forge, with an aperture through which bellows may have passed, and behind this is a room with a fireplace, table and benches all carved from stone.

The rooms on the left of the main passage are more elaborate and most contain furnishings carved out of sandstone. The first large room has a number of recesses with stone plinths which may have been used as beds. The next smaller space is almost entirely filled by a narrow stone table with benches on either side.

The next room is larger — about 15 feet long by 5 feet wide — and has its ceiling supported by a stone pillar. This room is popularly known as the 'drinking-parlour' and has a 10 feet long curving table at its centre with seats all round the edge. The base of the table is cut inwards with a 3-inch wide stone ledge left as a foot-rest, but the most unusual feature of the table is the 13 x 8 inch bowl-shaped cavity which has been carefully cut into the surface of the table. Two steps lead from the 'drinking parlour' to a 12-feet long narrow side passage which ends in a mass of masonry and which was probably another entrance to the cave. There is a further large room on the other side of this secondary passage.

At its far end, the main passage curves to the right and there is an entrance to a narrow tunnel about 3 feet high. The main parts of the cave have a ceiling height of around 6 feet. One theory is that the tunnel at one time provided a link to Craigmillar Castle.

Alexander Pennicuik, the 'burgess bard of Edinburgh', provided the following inscription, which is variously detailed as being carved in stone over the entrance and on a fireplace in the cave:

'Here is a house and shop hewn in this rock with my own hand' — George Paterson:

Upon the earth thrives villainy and woe,
But happiness and I do dwell below,
My hands hewed out this rock into a cell
Wherein from din of life I safely dwell.
On Jacob's pillow nightly lies my head,
My house when living and my grave when dead
Inscribe upon it when I'm dead and gone
I lived and died within my mother's womb.

There is now no sign of this inscription, but over the fireplace in the room behind the forge is a neatly carved oblong recess which may have contained the inscription on an inserted panel.

In 1897, F R Coles, Assistant Keeper of the National Museum of Antiquities of Scotland, investigated the cave and cast considerable doubt on whether Paterson had constructed it. Coles considered that 'the method of cutting the stone pointed to an origin much more remote than the 18th century and the substantial work involved in excavating the cave could not have been carried out by one man in five years'.

Coles also noted a number of narrow holes in the ceiling of the cave around the 'parlour'. He first considered that these were for ventilation, additional to the larger skylight openings in the roof; however, his alternative theory was that they were for 'bringing liquor down into the cave around the principal table at which, with its 'punch-bowl', carousals or secret political or masonic meetings were held'. It could be that Gilmerton Cave has a darker and more distant history than is popularly believed, although in one way that would be a pity . . . it makes such a good story as it is.

BLOODY MARY'S
CLOSE

The plague which so devastated the Old Town in 1645 took a particularly voracious toll of the inhabitants of Mary King's Close, killing most of them and leaving a legacy of superstitious fear which could border on uncomprehending terror.

The building of Royal Exchange, now the City Chambers, in 1753, was welcomed not least because it would 'obliterate the evil traditions of Mary King's Close in which the last dregs of the plague had secreted themselves and which had latterly been deserted by all but the powers of darkness'.

Mary King's Close had been a normal busy thoroughfare, dropping steeply down from the High Street to the old path around the Nor' Loch, until the plague struck. But then it was abandoned and the houses were sealed to prevent the spread of disease. For generations after, fear and superstition haunted the Close and it became a place of mystery and terror. Popular opinion persisted for many generations that if the houses were opened, the deadly pestilence would erupt again spreading disease and death. It was believed that those who were foolish enough to look through the windows of the houses after dark saw the spirits of the dead dancing in the moonlit rooms.

An account of Apparitions seen in a dwelling house in Mary King's Close given in the popular 1685 publication *Satan's Invisible World* describes spectral heads and ghostly cats and dogs.

Perhaps the most fascinating thing about Mary King's Close is that almost 350 years later and despite attempts to eradicate its 'vile traditions', a remnant of the infamous cobbled way remains virtually intact, deep in the foundations of the City Chambers. There is a baker's shop, hooks in a ceiling which were once used by a butcher to hang meat and houses complete with fireplace, shelved alcove and panelling. Despite regular visits by the 20th century's curious heritage-seekers, the plague has not re-emerged.

ROSS'S FOLLIES

St Bernard's House was once the principal house of Stockbridge. It was large and irregular with stones salvaged from the Old Town built into its walls. It stood in what is now Carlton Street and its owner was Mr Walter Ross, a solicitor whose knowledge of the law was 'solid and extensive'. He was 'eminently distinguished for his wit and humour' and well known for his collections of 'fine paintings and whimsical specimens of antiquity'.

One of these 'whimsical specimens' was an 8-feet-high block of stone intended for part of a colossal statue of Oliver Cromwell which was to have been erected in Edinburgh. The stone block had arrived in Leith with the news of Cromwell's death in 1658. The statue idea was scrapped and the stone was left neglected in Leith, but was always known as Oliver Cromwell. In 1788, Walter Ross arranged to have it moved to the grounds of St Bernards House. It was neglected after Ross's death and in the mid-19th century, 'Oliver Cromwell' was broken up for building stone.

Mr Ross was greatly troubled by nightly thefts of his collection of garden ornaments despite the fact that he advertised the presence of man-traps to deter thieves. Eventually he decided to obtain a human leg from the Royal Infirmary and had it dressed up in a stocking and shoe. It was then paraded through the town by the town-crier, who proclaimed that it had been found in Mr Walter Ross's garden at Stockbridge and was available for collection by its owner. The thefts stopped. Perhaps the technique could be adopted by today's Neighbourhood Watch schemes.

Ross also built in the grounds a curious tower which he used as a summer house. It was known as 'Ross's Folly' and stood on ground now occupied by the back garden of 10 Ann Street. The tower was about 40 feet high and had a single room at each of its two levels. The upper level featured a ceiling painting of a mythological scene and statues set in wall niches. The tower also had salvaged stones built into its walls, including four sculptured heads from the Old Cross of Edinburgh (which were sent to

Abbotsford in 1824 as a present for Sir Walter Scott), the font from St Ninian's Chapel on Leith Street and a sculpted eagle from excavations of a Roman site at Cramond.

Mr Ross died 'suddenly and unexpectedly and without any previous illness' in March, 1789. As a testimony to his 'wit and humour', it was widely rumoured that he choked during a fit of laughter.

After his death, the summerhouse was used as stables and later as a house by William Hutchison, street cleaner for the emerging Ann Street. The picturesque Folly was finally demolished in 1825 to make way for new building in Ann Street.

CALTON
CURIOSITIES

Calton Hill in the mid 18th century accommodated two popular places of entertainment. The uncompleted National Monument was enclosed by a high timber fence on which large signs advertised the attractions of 'Short's Popular Observatory' and 'Forrest's Statuary'. These establishments, one devoted to science and the other to the arts, occupied the space to the rear of the pillars of the Monument.

The domed building housed Miss Maria Theresa Short's 'Popular Observatory'. It featured a telescope, a camera obscura which projected a panoramic image of the surrounding area on a flat white table, and a Florascope, a form of kaleidoscope filled with coloured glass which could be moved to imitate the appearance of flowers.

Contemporary accounts refer to the scientific content of the 'Observatory' as 'farcical', but that did not detract from its popularity. The camera obscura moved to Castlehill in 1855, and was later acquired by Sir Patrick Geddes, the pioneer of town planning. It is still there, and, albeit slightly modified, it is still just as popular.

In 1832 Mr Robert Forrest, a Lanarkshire stonemason, built a hall adjoining 'Short's Observatory' in which he opened a 'grand exhibition of statuary'. Forrest was well known in Edinburgh for his statue of Viscount Melville which surmounts the 150 foot column in St Andrew Square. The original exhibits consisted of four large statues, including Robert the Bruce and the Duke of Wellington, but encouraged by public demand, this was ultimately increased to thirty. The collection included several life size equestrian groups depicting historic events, and statues of historic and traditional characters all 'executed with considerable skill and appreciation of art' by Mr Forrest. Each figure was cut from a single block of Craigleith stone and weighed five to eight tons.

The exhibition catalogue indicates that the statues were 'instructive without reference to their merits as works of arts and one of the great objects of attraction in Edinburgh'. This impression does not seem to have been universal, however, as there was a public outcry when it was proposed that the statues be placed as features in Princes Street Gardens. The collection was finally auctioned, in 1876, as 'decorations for gentlemen's policies, public parks or private gardens'.

DUDDINGSTON
CURLING SOCIETY

Curling has been a popular sport in Scotland since the 16th century. The Nor' Loch was Edinburgh's favourite venue, but when it was drained in the 18th century, Duddingston Loch began to attract the Edinburgh curlers.

The Duddingston Curling Society was formed in 1795 and it soon became the most important curling club in Scotland. Many hard winters in the early part of the 19th century provided perfect conditions and the sport boomed.

The membership fee for the Duddingston Society was three guineas and the club attracted the most distinguished curlers from all over Scotland. The Society had a number of officials, including a poet laureate. There was also a salaried officer, equipped with a ladder and ropes, who was responsible for the safety of curlers on the ice. The Society was the first to introduce a membership badge and members who failed to wear it on the ice were fined a shilling.

In 1803, the Society established the first code of rules for the game, 'to avoid disputes and ensure harmony amongst the members', and these were used as the basis for the rules of modern curling. They included fines for 'uttering oaths' and 'introducing a political subject into conversation'.

The Duddingston Curling Society flourished until 1853, when the game began to move indoors to artificial ice rinks.

MERCHISTON
PAGODA

Perhaps the strangest house ever built in Edinburgh was Rockville or, as it was variously known, The Pagoda, The Chinese House, Tottering Towers and Crazy Manor. Rockville, described as 'a building to delight every child who enjoys a fairy tale', stood at the corner of Napier Road and Spylaw Road in Merchiston and was built by Sir James Gowans in 1858 as his own home. Gowans was an architect, a railway engineer, a quarry owner, Edinburgh's Lord Dean of Guild and was knighted by Queen Victoria in 1886 for organising the International Exhibition in Edinburgh.

Rockville consisted of a three-storey house with a five-storey, 64-foot tower of Oriental influence. Its projecting stone dormers, decorative iron balusters, massive chimneys and ornate gables gave it an eerie Gothic appearance. The interior was spacious with hot water and gas in all the rooms and a kitchen with the motto 'Waste Not Want Not' carved in stone over the cooking range.

The acre of sunken garden included various statues, a bas-relief of Gowans as a master-mason, a stone table carved with gowans (Scots for wild daisies) and a gate lodge like a diminutive Hansel and Gretel house. The external walls of Rockville were built in a chequerboard pattern with a mosaic infill of coloured stones in a sandstone framework. The stones were selected from every quarry in Scotland, with samples from the Continent and China, and gave the building a rich effect of lightness and sparkle. The coloured granites produced a mainly reddish tint with highlights of green crystals of iron pyrites, an amethyst-like purple stone, silver mica and glittering quartz.

It was considered that Rockville represented 'the embodiment in stone of the same spirit which produced in literature the Gothic novel', but Gowans had 'no desire to create novelty'. Rockville to him was an experiment in building rationally using a modular grid system to produce an economic and aesthetically pleasing result. Hmm.

Proposals to demolish Rockville in the mid-1960s caused a public outcry and 2,500 signatures were collected on a petition to save it. Details of Rockville were even sent to the publicity manager of Disneyland suggesting that he might consider buying 'Edinburgh's Wonderhouse'. Rockville was finally demolished in 1966 and a block of flats constructed on the site. A hint of the romantic eccentricity of Rockville can still be seen in the surviving stone wall and gateposts.

THE GRAND EUROPEAN
Cabinet of Figures,

Madame Tussaud, Artist,

RESPECTFULLY informs the Gentry and Public of EDINBURGH.
her unrivalled Collection has just arrived here.

The full-length PORTRAIT-MODELS of their Most Gracious MAJESTIES

Geo. III. & Queen Charlotte,

THEIR ROYAL HIGHNESSES

THE PRINCE AND PRINCESS CHARLOTTE OF WALES,

Duke of York—Prince Charles Stuart;

LIEUTENANT-GENERAL SIR JOHN MOORE,

Admiral Lord Nelson,

GENERAL WASHINGTON.

Right Hon. Ch. Js. Fox—Right Hon. Wm. Pitt,

SIR FRANCIS BURDETT,

Right Hon. H. GRATTAN—Right Hon. J. P. CURRAN,
The Philanthropic Mr. ROSEBERRY, of Dublin,
Mons. TALLEYRAND—L'ABBE SIEYES,
COUNT DE LORGA,
The famous BARON TRENCK—The EMPRESS of FRANCE,
MADAME CATALANI, the celebrated Singer,
A SLEEPING CHILD—The ARTIST and her DAUGHTER.

AN EXACT LIKENESS OF THE BEAUTIFUL BUT UNFORTUNATE

Mary Queen of Scots.

JOHN KNOX, and JOHN WESLEY.

THE CELEBRATED

MRS. CLARKE.

A Coach and a Cannon,

Formed in Gold, Ivory, and Tortoise Shell,—to the Astonishment of the Spectator, is, with great Facility.

DRAWN by a FLEA!

The other Subjects composing this UNIQUE EXHIBITION, chiefly consisting of Portrait Characters,
in full Dress, as large as Life, correctly executed, may be classed as follows:

I. The late Royal Family of France, viz.

King, Queen, Princess Royal, and Dauphin; with M. de Clerie, Valet de Roi.

Celebrated Characters of the past and present Times, viz.

Henry IV. of France—Duc de Sully—Frederick the Great—M. de Voltaire—Pope Pius—J. J. Rousseau—
Dr. Franklin—Buonaparte—Madame Buonaparte—Archduke Charles—General Moreau—General
Kleber—Ex-Consul Cambaceres—Elfi Bey, and his Son; with a favourite Georgian Slave, and two
most beautiful Circassians.

II. Remarkable Characters:—Subjects, viz.

Madamoiselle Bruiser de Perigord, who foretold the French Revolution.
Princess de Lamballe, who was murdered by the Revolutionary Mob in Paris.
Madame du Barri, the Mistress of Louis XV. who was guillotined in Paris.
Madame St Amaranthe, guillotined for refusing to be the Mistress of Robespierre.
Charlotte Corde, who suffered by the guillotine for the Assassination of Marat.
Marat in the Agonies of Death, immediately after receiving the fatal Wound.
Heads of Robespierre, Fuquilier, de Thionville, Herbert, and Carriere, as they appeared after the guillotine
A Soldier of the French National Guards, in full Uniform.
An old Coquette, who teased her Husband's Life out.
One of Buonaparte's Mameluke Guards.——Madame St. Clair, the celebrated French Actress.

III. Curious and Interesting Relics, viz.

The SHIRT of HENRY IV. of France, in which he was assassinated by RIVAILLAC; and an accurate
Portrait of Rivaillac himself; with various original Documents relating to that Transaction.

A small Model of the original French Guillotine, with all its Apparatus;
and two Picturesque Models of the Bastile in Paris;
(In which Count de Lorga was confined Twenty Years:)

One representing that Fortress in an entire State, the other as destroying by the Revolutionists.

A real EGYPTIAN MUMMY, 3200 years old, in perfect Preservation.

Colonel Despard.

TUSSAUD'S
ACCLAIM

Madame Marie Tussaud first arrived in Britain in 1802 and, after a short stay in London, she brought her 'Grand European Cabinet of Figures' to Edinburgh. She arrived in Leith, with her strange collection of 70 life-size wax figures, on May 10, 1803 and, eight days later, opened her exhibition in Bernard's Rooms, Thistle Street.

The exhibits included 'exact replicas of the late Royal Family of France, a small model of the original French Guillotine and a 3299 years old Egyptian mummy, perfectly preserved'.

Fewer than 40 people visited the waxworks on the first day, but the handful of customers were 'astounded by the remarkably high standard of the models and the artistry of presentation'. Soon everyone wanted to see the wax portraits and business was so good that Madame Tussaud stayed in Edinburgh for six months. She noted that 'the Edinburgh show gives a great deal of pleasure and everyone is amazed at my figures'. This enthusiastic reception from the Edinburgh public established Madame Tussaud in Britain, and she never returned to France.

She visited Edinburgh several times after this and used the visits to keep her collection up to date. In 1829, she took the death-mask of Burke, just after he had been executed, and modelled Hare in prison. The figures of Burke and Hare are still included in the Chamber of Horrors at Madame Tussaud's in London.

THE ROYAL
ZOOLOGICAL
GARDENS

Edinburgh's first Royal Zoological Gardens opened to the public in August, 1840. They occupied six acres in East Claremont Street and were 'designed for securing safety as well as the favourable display of animals for the satisfaction of the spectators'.

The 1842 *Guide to the Royal Zoological Gardens* describes the Gardens as a 'most valuable institution of national importance forming an extensive and varied collection'. One report havered that the elephant exemplified the 'great utility of the Zoological Gardens in which the animal could be seen in living grandeur, it being so difficult to convey an adequate idea of this stupendous beast in words or even by drawings'. The specimen in the collection was a 'fine and imposing' eight year old male and visitors were particularly encouraged to admire 'that exquisite piece of mechanism, its lithe proboscis'.

The Bear Enclosure was a deep stone-lined pit with a pole in the centre by which 'Bruin would ascent to collect titbits offered by visitors'. The most 'striking and magnificent' exhibit was the 'wonderful and unique' skeleton of a whale which was 'astonishing in its ponderous proportions'. It measured 84 feet long and was the only perfect whale skeleton of its kind in existence. This 'stupendous production of nature' had been found floating in the sea, off Dunbar, by fishermen, dragged ashore and dissected on the beach by Dr Robert Knox and several assistants . . . probably rather a lot of assistants.

The Guide describes the Zoological Gardens as being 'well adapted to the healthful maintenance of the animals', but an independent account of the zoo refers to 'the wretched bear in a deep stone pit and the indescribable smell of the Monkey House, in which consumption carried off many of the inmates every season'. The only animals which are described as thriving are the polar bears which 'took abundance of playful exercise in a great bath and were unaffected by the inhospitable Edinburgh winters' and the elephant which 'obtained liberty and exercise from its ability to perambulate the grounds with dozens of juvenile visitors in its back'.

The animals were eventually so depleted from disease that the zoo closed in 1867.

A DAY AT THE MOVIES

The Mound has long been a focal point for outdoor performance in Edinburgh. During the first half of the 19th century, 'Geordie Boyd's Mud Brig' - the Mound - was a wide unkept space, described by Lord Cockburn as a 'receptacle of all things disreputable'.

On holidays and Saturdays, the site now occupied by the National Gallery of Scotland became the 'resort of low class traders and entertainers' who set up roulette tables, shooting galleries and coconut shies. Turkey Rhubarb (a guaranteed cure-all patent medicine), religious tracts, small dogs, spectacles and linnets in paper bags were among the goods on sale. Temporary shows were also allowed to use the site. These included Wombwell's Menagerie - which explains the elephant in the illustration - and in September, 1820, a six-foot high, 310-stone ox was exhibited to the public at the charge of 1/- for ladies and gentlemen and 6d for the working class (a rare example in Edinburgh of reverse privilege).

A more permanent show was the Rotunda, built in 1823 to house 'Barker's Panorama' in which Dioramas were shown. Dioramas were an early type of cinema involving a superior form of magic lantern display.

In its heyday, the Rotunda offered six one hour performances a day with commentary and musical accompaniment. The first public show consisted of a 'Grand Historical Panorama of the Battle of Waterloo', with music provided by a full military band. The most popular Diorama displays, drawing the largest audiences, were exhibitions of slides of ghostly apparitions and demons, the 19th century equivalent of horror films, and the comic effects of moving slides.

INTRODUCTORY
AND
HISTORICAL DESCRIPTION
OF
GORDON'S
BRITISH DIORAMAS,
INCLUDING
Saint George's Chapel, Windsor Castle,
WITH THE IMPOSING
FUNERAL OF GEORGE IV.;
THE TOWER OF LONDON,
AS SEEN DURING THE
RECENT CONFLAGRATION;
AND
THE AERONAUTIKON
OF
"THE GREAT NASSAU BALLOON,"
IN ITS
Aerial Voyage from London to Mayence in Germany;
•
COMPRISING
Views of London, its Public Buildings, Bridges, Shipping, &c. &c.—The Thames—Greenwich Hospital—Kent, "the Garden of England."—Rochester, and the Medway—Dover—The Channel—Calais—Cologne and its Cathedral—The Moselle River, and Magnificent Rhine, to Mayence in Germany.

NOW EXHIBITING
IN
GORDON'S BRITISH DIORAMA, EARTHEN MOUND, EDINBURGH.
Open from 1 till 4 o'Clock Afternoon, and 7 till 10 Evening.
THE WHOLE ACCOMPANIED WITH APPROPRIATE VOCAL AND INSTRUMENTAL MUSIC.

Admittance—Boxes, 1s. 6d.—Pit, 1s.—Gallery, 6d.
Children under 12 years of age, half-price to the Boxes and Pit.
N.B.--The Hall is Comfortably HEATED by Patent Stoves.

Educational 'documentary' displays, such as slides illustrating the movement of the planets and scenes of European cities with appropriate music and commentaries, were also a major attraction.

The Rotunda was demolished in 1850 to make way for the construction of the National Gallery.

ROCK HARMONICON

'A great novelty in musical instruments, the Rock Harmonicon' was exhibited in Edinburgh in 1842. The Harmonicon was originally developed by a stone-mason and consisted of 65 pieces of hard slate cut to different sizes, so that they formed a musical scale.

The stones were arranged horizontally in two tiers, resting on straw ropes supported by a wooden frame. Music was 'brought out of the Harmonicon by skilful manipulation'. This involved three performers striking the stones with wooden mallets.

The Harmonicon was 'no toy, but a perfect instrument and produced an agreeable effect, considering the nature and form of the substance'. The music obtained was 'particularly rich and melodious, some of the larger stones emitting a volume of sound equal to that of a deep-toned bell'.

The Edinburgh performances consisted of a selection of Scottish airs and melodies, but the 'most charming melody in the repertoire was Handel's *Harmonious Blacksmith,* which was more effective played on the Harmonicon than on the piano'. Nothing about rock music.

In the 1880s, the Harmonicon was taken to America. It is now preserved in a museum in Orange, New Jersey.

THE EDINBURGH TIME-GUN

A public demand arose in the Edinburgh of the 1850s for an accurate time service, but instead of a good clock the Time-Ball on the top of the Nelson Monument on Calton Hill was installed. The ball was wound up to the top of a pole and dropped by an electrical charge precisely at one o'clock. There were problems of course. The ball was not visible through 'mists or other optical obstructions' — or if you happened to be looking the other way at one o'clock. Undaunted, the public subscribed to the introduction of an audible time signal.

It was decided that the report of a cannon would be heard much more clearly than the stroke of a bell and the Royal Artillery provided a 94 pounder gun at Edinburgh Castle. Experiments with other guns had resulted in the breakage of nearby windows, and doubtless many unrecorded heart failures. The cannon was connected to time-keeping equipment at the Observatory on Calton Hill by a 4,200 feet long insulated cable which operated a mechanical trigger to fire the gun at exactly the right time. The single span of the cable was the longest in the world and the clock was kept to the precise time by astronomical observations.

The first public firing of the Time-Gun was arranged for the 5 June, 1861 and 300 members of the public, who had taken an interest in the project, and other distinguished guests were invited to attend at the Calton Hill Observatory. The excitement was considerable amongst the invited audience as they awaited the simultaneous drop of the Time-Ball and flash of the cannon at the Castle; the sound of the gun was expected four seconds later due to the distance between Castle and Observatory.

Precisely at one o'clock, the Time-Ball dropped and everyone 'held their breath, strained their eyes and bent their ears towards the Castle'. After a long interval, to the 'considerable disappointment of the audience and embarrassment of the organisers', there was no sign of anything in the way of a time signal from the Castle and the invited guests were invited back the following day. The problem was a faulty detonator in the cannon.

After its false start, it became well-known for its dependability and remains a daily feature of Edinburgh life.

BLONDIN'S
SECOND AND LAST FETE.

THIS EVENING
—

EXPERIMENTAL GARDEN EDINBURGH
INVERLEITH Row
—

When in Addition to his other
MARVELLOUS FEATS
HE WILL PROPEL A WHEELBARROW ACROSS
THE ENTIRE LENGTH OF THE ROPE
STAND UPON HIS HEAD
WALK ENVELOPED IN A SACK, AND EYES
BANDAGED

With other of his
NIAGARA EXPLOITS
Performed by no other Human Being
—

And will also
CARRY A MAN UPON HIS BACK
As given before H.R.H. THE Prince of Wales
At **NIAGARA FALLS**
September, 1860
—

The BAND of the 26th REGIMENT will attend by the kind
permission of Colonel Carey and Officers
—

PRICES OF ADMISSION
Tickets, One Shilling and Sixpence; Grand Stand 5s;
Family Tickets, admitting Four to Grand Stand 10s.
—

Gates open at 5. Band Performance at Half past 5.
Blondin's Ascension about half past 6.
—

Tickets to be had of Paterson & Sons, 27 George Street,
and Robertson & Co., Princes Street.

INVERLEITH
DAREDEVIL

When Charles Blondin, the 'Daredevil Wirewalker', arrived in Edinburgh, he was already a legendary figure due to his tightrope crossing of the Niagara Falls.

His two appearances in Edinburgh were at the Royal Botanic Garden, then known as the Experimental Gardens, in Inverleith Row, in September 1861. A grandstand was erected for the performances and, long before the advertised time of Blondin's arrival the arena was packed with 'an assemblage of 5,000 spectators, to witness Blondin's world famous feats of skill and daring'.

He immediately 'grasped his balancing pole and, after a few cautious steps, he literally ran across the rope in the most easy and apparently nonchalant manner imaginable'. He performed a number of acrobatic feats the second time on the rope: lying on his back, standing on one leg, hanging by his legs, turning a somersault and finally 'producing a thrill by standing on the rope on his head'. All this was done with 'apparent unconcern, as freely as though he were on the ground'.

Blondin was then blindfolded and a canvas sack, reaching to his knees, was put over his head, leaving only his arms free to use the balancing pole. 'After a few feigned slips, which were greeted by the painful apprehension of the crowd, he proceeded on his course steadily, as if he were walking on a broad plank close to the ground'. His arrival at the other end of the rope 'produced a sigh of relief, in addition to great applause'.

In his final performance, he 'carried on his back, with careless freedom, the same gentleman that he did at the Falls of Niagara. The conclusion of each of his exploits was greeted with outbursts of applause, and this final act astonished the multitude who had assembled and was met with audible expressions of gratification that it was safely completed'.

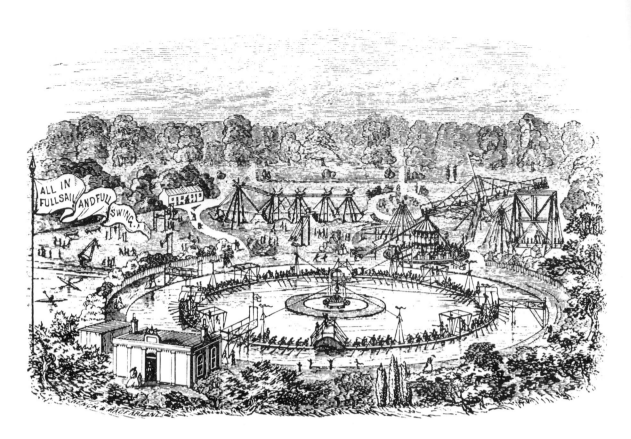

THE
ROYAL PATENT GYMNASIUM,
THE NEW AND INCREASING WONDER OF EDINBURGH,
ROYAL CRESCENT PARK, adjoining Scotland Street Station.

THE PATENT ROTARY BOAT,
'GREAT SEA SERPENT,'
Is seated for 600 Rowers, embarking and disembarking Passengers at Four different Piers, at opposite sides of the Island, at the same time ! ! !

THE PATENT VELOCIPEDE
PADDLE MERRY-GO-ROUND
Is 160 feet in circumference, and can accommodate 600 Persons.

THE PATENT
Giant's Sea-Saw 'CHANG'
Is 100 feet long by 7 feet broad, and can accommodate 200 Persons, elevating them to a height of 50 feet.

THE PATENT
SELF-ADJUSTING TRAPEZE
Enables Gymnasts to Swing by the hands a distance of 130 feet from one Trapeze to the other.

THE PATENT
COMPOUND PENDULUM SWING
Holds about 100 persons, and is kept in motion by those upon it.

There are also interesting varieties of
SMALL BOATS AND CANOES ON THE PONDS
Propelled by various novel methods.

THE PRINCE ALFRED WRECK ESCAPE;
Also to be seen Specimens of
SWIMMING STOCKINGS, STILTS, & STOUPS

The Giant's Strides, Giant's Leap, Horizontal and Rotary Ladders, Parallel Bars, Vaulting Poles, Sloping-Sliding Ropeways, Stilts, Quoits, Balls, etc. etc.

Admission, 6d.; Children under 12, 3d. Season Tickets at moderate prices.
Schools and Institutions, en masse, Half-price.

A MILITARY or other BAND on Saturday or Holiday Afternoons, Weather Permitting.

THE ROYAL PATENT
GYMNASIUM

A small advertisement in the local newspapers of July, 1865, announced that the Royal Patent Gymnasium — 'The New Wonder of Edinburgh' — was 'In Full Sail and Full Swing'.

It was the brainchild of John Cox, businessman and philanthropist of Gorgie House, Edinburgh. Cox had decided that Edinburgh citizens required somewhere to exercise and improve their physical fitness, and conceived the idea of using a large sheltered area at Canonmills Loch as an open-air pleasure-ground for the 'promotion of healthful recreation'.

Canonmills Loch was an extensive area of water in a natural hollow between Eyre Place and Royal Crescent, to the north-east of Edinburgh's Georgian New Town. It was shallow and marshy and provided a habitat for water-fowl and a species of fighting perch sufficiently numerous to attract anglers.

The surroundings of the loch were rural until the early 19th century when the New Town began to encroach. Before the middle of the century, the loch was drained and in 1847, railway platforms were erected at the eastern end of the loch area — the new Scotland Street

CANONMILLS LOCH AND HOUSE, 1830. (*From an Oil Painting by J. Kidd.*)

Station, first stop on the line to Granton which descended a steep tunnel all the way from Princes Street.

Strange-looking wooden structures began to appear on the grounds adjoining the railway in 1864. Their function must have been a puzzle to passers-by. No doubt many theories circulated about the proposed use of the site, none of them as bizarre as the truth.

The Gymnasium was successful from the start and, for the modest entrance charge of 6d, the visitor was offered a wide selection of 'ingenious contraptions affording amusement and healthful bodily exercise'. The scale was extravagant.

One of the main attractions was the Patent Rotary Boat, or Great Sea Serpent. This remarkable device involved a large circular pond with a post mounted in the middle. Long wire spokes radiated out from the post to the wooden structure of the boat, which was 471 feet round and could accommodate 600 people. Passengers sat in the apparatus and rowed the boat-serpent in fixed circles. When the equipment was fully manned, the whole thing travelled round at a speed 'equal to that of a small steam boat'.

The Rotary Boat was such an important feature of the Patent Gymnasium that it had a musical composition, a grand march entitled *The Great Sea Serpent* dedicated to it. This was written by a certain C Laubach and was first performed at the Gymnasium by the Band of The Edinburgh Rifle Volunteers on July 29, 1865.

Another popular piece of amusing apparatus was Chang — The Giant's Sea-Saw — an alleyway 100 feet long by 7 feet wide, mounted on a pivot and brought into play by any number of people, up to 200, running up the inclined side of the structure. The ends of the see-saw travelled through an arc of 50 feet and the final shock on the downward action was so great that tanks of water were required to absorb the movement. Fitted above the fulcrum of the structure was a giant figure — Chang — which swung slowly to each side in harmony with the motion of the balancing beam.

A major problem with the Sea-Saw seems to have been that of 'equalising the oscillation to prevent uncomfortable jolting' whilst people were getting on and off.

In another part of the park was a wooden circular catwalk above which moved an endless chain of 144 leather saddles. Here patrons sat and propelled themselves around the catwalk with their feet. Inside this moving belt was a two-storey glass structure where spectators could sit while they admired the 'invigorating motion of the machine'.

Seats were also fitted alongside the saddles, so that passengers could jump on and 'enjoy the rotary action without any effort on their part'. Further muscular recreation was provided by a Velocipede Merry-Go-

Round — 160 feet in circumference and self-propelled by its 600 riders; the Patent Compound Pendulum Swing, which was self-adjusting, so that the seats remained horizontal no matter what height they swung to; and the Giant's Stride — a 40-feet round wheel, mounted on a greased tree trunk, with chains hanging around its circumference for customers to grab and swing on.

More conventional facilities and pastimes at the Gymnasium included vaulting, climbing poles, stilts, quoits, springboards, bowls and swimming-baths. And, as if all that hadn't done enough damage, you could always hire a boneshaker.

In winter, a large part of the grounds was turned into an ice rink and illuminated at night for skating carnivals.

In its time, the Royal Patent Gymnasium was the only resort of its kind in the country and one of the great sights of the city. Unfortunately, its popularity seems to have ebbed by the end of the century and the site became a football ground. It is a great pity that there is no remaining evidence of this wonderfully eccentric Victorian playground.

WOMBWELL'S ROYAL MENAGERIE

Was there ever a more remarkable auction sale than that which took place in the old Waverley Market in Edinburgh on April 9, 1872? For sale was Wombwell's Royal Menagerie, 'a famous collection of wild beasts, birds and reptiles which had delighted the populace of the United Kingdom for four generations'.

Wombwell's Menagerie was one of the earliest and largest travelling zoological collections in Britain and 'did more to familiarise the minds of the masses of the people with the creatures of the forest than all the books of natural history ever printed'. The menagerie appeared annually in the Grassmarket, arriving in a long parade of animals through the city.

The collection was established by George Wombwell in 1805 and was renowned for the beauty and variety of the animals. Wombwell travelled with the show until his death in 1850. It was run by his wife until 1866, when it was inherited by Alexander Fairgrieve of Edinburgh, a nephew of Wombwell, who conducted it until the auction sale.

The auction of the menagerie animals was such a novel event that a

WOMBWELL'S ROYAL MENAGERIE
PAVILION, WAVERLEY MARKET, EDINBURGH

Mr FAIRGRIEVE respectfully intimates that the whole MENAGERIE, comprising the unrivalled collection of BLACK MANED LIONS ,TIGERS ,LEOPARDS. Magnificent Performing ELEPHANTS, CAMELS and DROMEDARIES, with the whole of the other WILD BEASTS, BIRDS and REPTILES also a ROAN PONY, very fast, with Trap and Harness, WAGGONS, TRAPPINGS, &c., &c., will be SOLD by AUCTION, by Mr BUIST, on TUESDAY, APRIL 9 , 1872. Mr Fairgrieve would draw the attention of Ladies and Gentlemen to this sale, as there are a number of Beautiful Specimens of PARROTS, COCKATOOS, and MACAWS. These birds have been thoroughly acclimatised and are very suitable for pets. There are also several Beautiful Pet Monkeys and other Smaller Animals.

The Collection will remain open until the day of the sale. Admission, 1s each; Children, 6d each; Working Classes, 6d each. No extra charge for feeding. Admission on day of Sale 2s 6d each.

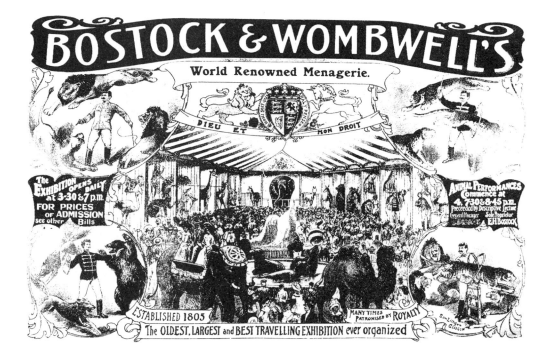

large audience gathered in Princes Street to see the last appearance of the elephants, camels and other animals as part of Wombwell's Menagerie. The sale had 'excited considerable international attention' and the capacity crowd in the Waverley Market included 'well-known naturalists, circus proprietors, and representatives of zoos in Britain, America and France'.

The animals offered for sale included various breeds of monkey and baboon, a wombat, porcupines, hyenas, a gnu, boa constrictors, zebras, a variety of bears, two elephants, eleven lions, a Bengal tiger, seven camels and three 'beautiful glossy' leopards.

The sale started with the monkeys, which were recommended as 'lively, frisky, intelligent and clean pets', and competition was brisk for some of the rarer species. The vultures, pelicans, emu and condor were sold to dealers while the parrots and cockatoos 'provided lively interest amongst local bird fanciers'. One cockatoo fetched £8 due to its excellent talking abilities. The Earl of Rosebery bought a racoon for £1, and the Tasmanian Devil was sold for 65 shillings.

There was fierce competition among dealers for the larger animals such as the polar and Tibetan bears and the performing elephant. 'Hannibal', a black-maned lion, the 'handsomest and largest specimen in Britain', was purchased for £270 by Bristol Zoo.

Many of the animals were sold for considerably more than their market value, and the total amount realised for the ninety unusual lots was £2,900.

THE GREAT
LAFAYETTE

The Great Lafayette was one of the most popular entertainers of the early 20th century, but his two-week season in Edinburgh in May, 1911 was extraordinary even by his standards. His mystifying illusions and elaborate quick-changes, were presented in the most lavish and spectacular act ever seen in the music-halls. He was the highest paid entertainer in the theatre, receiving a weekly fee of £350.

Lafayette had an eccentric lifestyle. He lived as a bachelor recluse with a small cross-bred terrier, named Beauty, which he had been given by Harry Houdini. The dog slept on velvet cushions, dined at the table with Lafayette, had a collar of pure gold studded with diamonds. The radiator ornament on Lafayette's limousine was a metal statuette of the dog. Lafayette's London home and his private railway carriage had special rooms for the dog, fitted with dog-sized settees and miniature porcelain baths. A plaque over the entrance to Lafayette's London home was inscribed: 'The more I see of men the more I love my dog'.

Lafayette opened a two-week season at the Empire Theatre of Varieties in Nicolson Street on May 1. Four days later Beauty died of apoplexy, caused by over-feeding. Lafayette was grief-stricken, and had the dog laid out on a silk pillow surrounded by lilies in his rooms in the Caledonian Hotel. Lafayette had Beauty embalmed and was given permission to have the dog interred at Piershill Cemetery, provided he agreed to be buried in the same place. Meanwhile the show went on.

On Tuesday May 9, 3000 spectators packed the Empire Theatre for Lafayette's second evening performance. Lafayette's act was the finale of the show. He entered, to a trumpet fanfare, dressed in a satin costume and proceeded to shake dozens of birds from a sequined cloth, finally producing a goat from the folds of the material. His act continued with 'other remarkable illusions and elaborate scenarios in which he demonstrated his habit of changing identity with his many assistants'.

The finale was the 'Lion's Bride' which involved the use of tapestries, cushions, tents and curtains to create an Oriental setting. An

African lion paced restlessly in a cage while fire-eaters, jugglers and contortionists performed. A young woman in Oriental dress walked slowly on stage and entered the cage. When she was inside, the lion roared and reared up ready to pounce. The animal skin was then suddenly ripped away to reveal The Great Lafayette who had mysteriously changed places with the lion.

As The Great Lafayette took his bow a lamp fell amongst the scenery which instantly caught fire. A mass of flame shot over the footlights to the stalls. The audience, now accustomed to unusual effects, were slow to recognise the danger. Only when the fire curtain was rapidly lowered did they hurry to the exits. By this time the stage was an inferno. It took three hours to bring the fire under control, and eleven people died. They included members of the orchestra, stage hands, a midget in the act called Little Joe, Alice Dale, a tiny 15-year-old girl who operated a scene-stealing mechanical teddy-bear and the Great Lafayette.

Eyewitness reports claimed Lafayette had escaped but had returned in an attempt to save his horse. A charred body, dressed in Lafayette's costume, was found near the stage, but a further search of the basement revealed another body, this one with the diamond rings which Lafayette always wore. The first man was one of the doubles that Lafayette often used in his act.

On May 14, 1911 the streets of Edinburgh were thronged with spectators to see his ashes moved from a funeral parlour in Morrison Street to Piershill Cemetery. The funeral was described as 'one of the most extraordinary internments of modern times'. The first car in the long cortège was Lafayette's silver-grey Mercedes, the sole passenger being 'Mabel', a Dalmatian hound. There was great ceremonial at the Cemetery, as Beauty's coffin was opened and Lafayette's ashes placed beside the dog. Harry Houdini sent a floral representation of Beauty to the funeral.

The grave, with memorial stones to Beauty and The Great Lafayette, can be seen on a grassy mound just inside the Portobello Road entrance to Piershill Cemetery.

BUFFALO BILL'S

WILD WEST EXHIBITION
AND CONGRESS OF ROUGH RIDERS

Colonel William F Cody, alias Buffalo Bill, brought his 'Wild West Exhibition and Congress of Rough Riders of the World' to Edinburgh in August, 1904. The week of performances was staged on a large area of open ground at Gorgie Road and special trains were provided to the nearby Gorgie Station.

The show was billed as the 'crowning equestrian spectacle of the ages' and involved performers from all over the world; but retained a 'predominant flavour of the picturesque and adventurous life of the Wild West'. The company was large — 800 men and women with 500 horses — and required three trains for transportation.

The two hour performances commenced with an 'imposing review' of Buffalo Bill's Rough Riders: a hundred Red Indians — 'Red men, chiefs, warriors, squaws and papooses with feather head-dresses, long spears, bead jackets and uttering discordant war cries' — British Lancers, U S Cavalry, Cossacks, Bedouin Arabs, Gauchos from Argentina, Mexican Vaqueros, Japanese Mounted Troops and American Cowboys. Finally Buffalo Bill appeared and was greeted with rapturous applause, 'a tribute to his fame and daring as a skilful frontier scout and his success as organiser of the night's entertainment'.

The show continued with an exhibition of drills by the US Cavalry and British Lancers; acrobatics, wire-walking and juggling by Arab and Japanese performers; a war-dance by a large troupe of Indians and 'feats of equestrian skill' by the Cossacks.

A large section of the company re-enacted 'Wild West Incidents' such as the Battle of the Little Big Horn, a stage-coach hold-up, a cattle round-up, riding bucking broncos and attacks on a wagon train and settler's hut. The 'raiding Indians and defending cowboys did their work with abundant noise and bustle, and with spirit and energy which made the scenes intensely realistic'.

Buffalo Bill demonstrated his shooting skills by hitting small balls thrown in the air while he was riding on horseback, and Johnny Baker, a young American marksman, 'even when standing on his head brought down clay pigeons with his rifle'.

GREIG'S
RIDING SCHOOL

In the mid-19th century, one of the most 'notable establishments' in Edinburgh was Greig's Riding School. The Riding School was located in the Royal Amphitheatre, which stood on Nicolson Street near Nicolson Square.

Lessons were given in the 'polite art of Riding with ease and grace, on the most moderate terms in Scotland' and pupils were drawn from the sons and daughters of the best people in the city.

Mr Greig, the riding-master, was a familiar figure on the South Side of Edinburgh and was known as 'Ghostly Greig'. He is described as a 'tall, striking man, always dressed with the most scrupulous neatness in approved riding garments'.

CAMERA OBSCURA

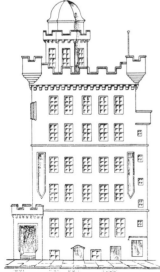

In 1855, Maria Theresa Short moved her exhibition of scientific instruments from Calton Hill to new premises at the top of Castlehill. The building, which was traditionally believed to be the town mansion of the 'Laird of Cockpen', had been transformed by the addition of two floors into Short's Observatory. Exhibits included 'a powerful galvanic machine which gives shocks of any power, a Fairy Fountain of Electric Water and a Wonderful Electric Boy'. The main attraction, however, was the Camera Obscura, a periscope device of mirrors and lenses which throws a moving image onto a reflective table.

In 1892, the building was purchased by Patrick Geddes and there followed the most interesting period in the building's history. Geddes was officially a botanist and biologist, but was involved in a multitude of other activities, and is perhaps best remembered for his work in the field of town planning. There are many places throughout the world that bear traces of the influence of Patrick Geddes. In Edinburgh he was responsible for setting up the first student hostel in Scotland; designing the Zoo; building Ramsay Garden, as co-operative housing, and improvement schemes in the Old Town.

Geddes intended to transform the building into a 'place of outlook and a type-museum as a key to a better understanding of Edinburgh and its region, but also to help people get a clear idea of its relation to the world at large'.

Geddes believed that a tour of the Outlook Tower should begin at the top of the building on the flat roof terrace where a general idea of the Edinburgh region and 'one of the great views of the world' could be seen. The camera obscura then provided a different view of the outside environment, in the 'miniature-like perfection of detail' reflected in the moving image on the screen. After this 'lesson in the art of seeing' it was felt that 'quiet reflection and meditation on the many new impressions which had been gathered' would be required, so a small darkened room with a single chair was provided.

Each lower storey of the Tower was devoted to exhibits and collections of material relating to the World, Europe, Language, Scotland and Edinburgh. Exhibits included an Episcope, which provided a view of the world 'as if it were suddenly to become transparent beneath one's feet', a Hollow Globe and a Celestial Sphere. All of these were intended to show the relation of the world to its surroundings in the Universe.

The Edinburgh Room had a relief model of the city and illustrations showing its architectural development. In the Scotland Room the evolution of the Scottish nation was traced by a large floor map.

The Outlook Tower was at its best up to 1914, when Patrick Geddes was most often there. It retained its educational function for a number of years and a larger camera was installed in 1945. The Camera Obscura remains a popular tourist attraction, but it is unfortunate that there remains no clear recognition of its association with Patrick Geddes, the 'father of modern town planning'.

WORLD WONDER

Thirty thousand people thronged the Meadows on May 6, 1886 when Prince Albert Victor opened the International Exhibition of Industry, Science and Art. The Exhibition building was an imposing structure comprising a Grand Hall, fronting the main entrance at Brougham Place, with a range of double courts extending eastwards and arranged on either side of a central corridor. The Grand Hall had a 120-feet high central dome decorated with signs of the Zodiac, an impressive collection of statues around the entrance, a Grand Organ and orchestra platform and could hold 10,000 people.

By the opening day, 12,000 season tickets, at a guinea each had been sold.

Over 20,000 exhibits illustrated the 'material progress of the age' and there were 1,725 works of art in the fine art galleries. The list of items displayed included 'educational appliances; Italian furniture and marble; violins from Prague; Turkish embroidery; illustrations of mining, pottery, sugar-refining, sea industries, paper-making, printing; and railway, tram-way and other vehicular appliances'. The Women's Industries display ranged through Belgian glove-making, Fair Isle, Shetland and Icelandic knitting, Irish linen and artificial fly production.

The grounds were laid out with walks, rockery, fountain and bandstand. The principal open-air attractions were the electric railway which ran between the main Brougham Place entrance and Middle Meadow Walk; the working man's model dwelling-house, which included the most modern appliances for sanitation and convenience; and the refreshment rooms, both temperance and otherwise. The Exhibition buildings and grounds were lit by 3,200 electric lamps in the largest illumination scheme ever attempted in Scotland.

One of the most popular features of the Exhibition was the 'most novel and picturesque' Old Edinburgh Street consisting of various buildings which existed in Edinburgh during the 17th-century. The Street was entered through a replica of the Netherbow Port, and the buildings were arranged to form a street typical of Old Edinburgh with a short High Street, market place, mercat cross, two closes and a copy of the Old Tolbooth. Architectural styles were apparently reproduced with 'great fidelity and the imitation of old stonework was particularly marvellous'. The ground floors were laid out as forty-four shops and workshops in which attendants dressed in 17th-century costumes sold souvenirs of the Exhibition.

Queen Victoria visited in August, 1886. It was originally intended to retain the Grand Hall and the model dwelling-houses, after the exhibition closed on October 30, but an Act of Parliament forbids all permanent buildings within the Meadows, and they were demolished. Surviving relics include the Masons' Memorial Pillars and Prince Albert Victor Sundial, both at the west end of the Meadows; the Brassfounders' Pillar, now in Nicolson Square Gardens; the six Doulton tile panels depicting great inventors, displayed in the Café Royal; and the whale jawbone arch on Melville Drive.

SCOTTISH NATIONAL EXHIBITION

The Scottish National Exhibition was held in Saughton Park, Edinburgh in 1908. The aims of the Exhibition were to exemplify all that was best in Art, Science, Literature and Industry from 'His Majesty's Dominions'. A new station was built by the North British Railway Company on the main line adjoining the Exhibition, to bring visitors from Waverley Station.

The Palace of Industries covered an area of 100,000 square feet, with an ornamental tower of 125 feet at each end. The exhibits were of an 'exceptionally high-class character, comprising the following sections: Scottish, Irish, English, Dutch, Japanese, Italian and Canadian, besides sections devoted to Education, Transport and Women's Work.'

The Machinery Hall featured printing, lithography, shipping, mining, electric, gas, steam, water, sewage disposal, baking and confectionery.

The Fine Art Galleries housed the best of Scottish art and a collection of 'rare and historic exhibits that must appeal to every Scotsman, and should prove intensely interesting to visitors from all parts of the world'. One gallery was set aside for 'one of the most complete collections of rare and valuable relics appertaining to the Highlands and Islands of Scotland ever brought together'. Among the exhibits were regimental colours, old clan tartans, Gaelic manuscripts, claymores and — inevitably — locks of Bonnie Prince Charlie's hair.

The Music and Conference Hall was 'a most striking building, circular in shape, with prettily decorated outside walls and four ornamental towers'. It included 'a striking novelty in the shape of a fairy fountain which sprays water from hundreds of varying jets and with limelight shed upon it from overhead at different angles produces a most beautiful scene, that in point of colour rivals the rainbow and a handsome organ with patent tubular pneumatic action and blowers'. Understatement was not the order of the day.

The Winter Garden was a 'delightful place for large parties to enjoy the cup that cheers' — tea, alas — and can still be seen on Balgreen Road.

ALEX. FERGUSON'S KIOSK
at the SCOTTISH NATIONAL EXHIBITION.
The Upper Part represents the City Arms. The Lower Part, a Rock Temple.
The Whole,

EDINBURGH ROCK
REGD TRADE MARK № 2217

SEVENPENCE
RETURN

The Marine Gardens, 'one of the most notable outdoor attractions of Edinburgh', were opened to the public in 1909. The Gardens were a huge entertainment complex, stretching a quarter of a mile westwards of King's Road, Portobello. Admission was 7d, including return rail fare from Waverley, and three quarters of a million people visited the Gardens in its first year.

The Empress Ballroom was the main building, flanked by a concert hall and skating rink. There were all-star variety shows every day in the concert hall with some of the best vaudeville acts of the time. The included: Mr John Cronow, 'the world's greatest facial expert giving impersonations of past and present celebrities' and groups such as the Humoresks, the Dandies and the Enterpeans which provided a mixture of comedy sketches, monologues, song, dance and burlesque.

The amusement park in the Gardens had a scenic railway, a joy wheel, a mountain slide, river caves and a maze, which 'recalled the complexities of the famous model at Hampton Court'. The main attraction of the amusement park was the Somali Village in which seventy natives of Somaliland lived in a small compound and provided entertainment for visitors by performing fights armed with spears. This was 'all carried through to the accompaniment of uncouth cries, the beating of the tom-tom and the shrill piping of the leading musician'.

EDINBURGH MARINE GARDENS
SKATING RINK.

Friday Evening, July 29th—7 to 11.

First Gymkhana of the Season.

❧ PROGRAMME. ❧

1.	Two-Step,	"Yip-i-addy-i-ay,"	All Skate.
2.	Valse,	"Arcadians,"	All Skate.
3.	Two-Step,	"Light of Heart,"	Partners Only.
4.	Valse,	"Remembrance,"	All Skate.
5.	Gentlemen's Hoop Race.		
6.	Two-Step,	"I can't reach that top note,"	All Skate.
7.	Ladies' Balloon Race.		
8.	Waltz,	"Warbling of Birds,"	Partners Only.
9.	Gentlemen's Three-Legged Race.		
10.	Musical Chairs for Gentlemen only.		
11.	Ladies' Shopping Race.		
12.	Waltz,	"Fugi San,"	All Skate.
13.	Gentlemen's Half Mile Amateur Race.		
14.	Ladies' Half Mile Handicap Race.		
15.	Two-Step,	"Dollar Princess,"	Ladies Only.
16.	Gentlemen's Egg and Spoon Race.		
17.	Waltz,	"La Rinka,"	All Skate.
18.	Gentlemen's and Ladies' Potatoe Race.		
19.	Partners' Half Mile Race.		
20.	Two-Step,	"I do like to be beside the Seaside,"	All Skate.
21.	Waltz,	"Mondaine,"	Partners Only.
22.	Waltz,	"Pantomine Song,"	All Skate.

"God Save the King."

Conductor— Mr J. V. CAINE.

Manager— S. W. HELLMAN.

Watch our Advertisements for the Two Mile Amateur Roller Skating Race for the Championship of Scotland.

Other attractions consisted of performances by well known bands and musicians in the band court; a billiard saloon which featured demonstration matches by T Aiken, the Scottish champion; Hibbert's Electric Pictures; a social club for the use of regular visitors to the Gardens; skating gymkhanas in the ice rink and a sports arena for football and motor cycle racing.

The heyday of the gardens was short-lived. The site became a barracks for troops in the First World War and was used for a variety of other purposes over the years. It is now a bus depot.

EDINBURGH
MARINE GARDENS

COCONUT TAM

Edinburgh's best known street character in the latter part of the 19th century was 'Coconut Tam'. He had a regular stance on the High Street where he sold fruit, vegetables and especially coconuts. His 'thin-voiced' street cry was 'Coco-nit! Coco-nit! Come an' buy, ha'penny the bit'.

His real name was Thomas Simpson and he lived in Potterrow behind the Empire Theatre. He is described as a 'thin, humpy wee man with outsize lugs supporting a frayed bowler hat which jauntily displayed a large sprig of heather'.

PORTY POOL

For many years one of the main tourist attractions in Portobello was the open-air swimming baths. The baths were formally opened on May 30, 1936 by Lord Provost Gumley in front of a capacity crowd of 6,000.

The Pool was designed by the city engineer's department to the Olympic standards of the time. The pool area was 330 feet long by 150 feet wide, and varied in depth from one foot to six feet two inches at the deep end. Six thousand spectators could be accommodated, with 2,000 seats available under the most modern design of cantilevered stand, and there were lockers provided for 1284 swimmers. The one and a half million gallons of water required to fill the pool was filtered sea water heated to a temperature of 68° Fahr by steam from the adjacent power station.

The pool's great innovation was the first ever wave-making machine in Scotland. This consisted of four 24-feet long pistons mounted in a chamber at the deep end of the pool, which were arranged to send 3-feet high wages in three possible directions. These artificial waves were so dramatic that the machine was only operated after a warning had been given.

In the pre-war years the Pool was extremely popular. Its record was 18,000 people in one day. Band music was often specially relayed from Princes Street Gardens, and there was a choice of bather's snack bar, restaurant or open-air tea garden.

The Pool was closed for six years during the Second World War and had to be camouflaged to stop it being used as a landmark by enemy planes. It re-opened in June, 1946 and remained popular for a number of years, but it fell into a long and controversial decline, and was finally demolished in the late 1980s.

PORTY PIER

In 1869, Parliament passed a Bill for the erection of a pier at Portobello. It was felt that a pier was required to add to the variety of attractions available to visitors and to 'develop Portobello as a place of pleasure and enjoyment to its inhabitants and to the many visitors from Edinburgh and from afar'.

Sir Thomas Bouch (who was later responsible for the ill-fated Tay Bridge) designed the pier and it was completed in 1871 at a cost of £10,000. It stretched 1,250 feet into the sea from near the foot of Bath Street.

The opening ceremony, on May 23, 1871, was performed by Lord Provost Wood and was witnessed by a 'great assembly' of spectators. It was claimed that the Portobello Pier was the first of its kind ever built in Scotland and second to none in the country.

The Pier was a popular promenade and few people 'grudged the nominal toll exacted for the pleasure of the bracing walk'. Other attractions on the Pier included 'a well conducted tea room and restaurant; a small camera obscura which provided views of the sands, sea and coastline; and a concert hall at the far end which was not well patronised in cold or wet weather'. Sailings to Elie, North Berwick, the Bass Rock and the Isle of May left from Portobello Pier during the summer.

Frequent structural repairs were needed due to the corrosive action of the sea water on the iron supports and it was finally removed in 1917.

Memories of the original Portobello Pier were revived in the 1930s, when a group of private entrepreneurs set up a company to build a new pier in Portobello to 'renew its claim as being the Brighton of the North'. Plans were drawn up for a pier with a restaurant, shops and concert hall. A 1,000-feet projection into the sea was planned to provide sufficient depth of water at the pier head for pleasure steamers. It was hoped that work would start in 1940, but the War changed all that and the scheme was never revived.

THE
KINETIC
SCULPTURE

Edinburgh's penchant for bizarre public gesture finally took leave of its senses when in September, 1973, the most spectacular part of Edinburgh's Christmas decorations was announced as being a permanent 80-feet high 'spiral of kinetic art on a traffic roundabout at Picardy Place'.

The sculpture was designed by Roger Dainton. It was a metal tower on which were fixed 96 coloured light tubes linked to electrical circuits which were controlled by a wind vane. The idea was that the intensity, variation and rate of change of the lights would be determined by wind speed and direction, and that this would result in 'more than a million light pattern combinations'. The final cost of the sculpture — £11,000 — was shared between the Scottish Arts Council and Edinburgh Corporation.

The switching-on ceremony on December 22, was attended by 'Mr Dainton, the designer, some council officials and a few bedraggled rain-soaked Christmas shoppers'. But this was the era of the three day week and power restrictions — the infamous 'Winter of Discontent' — and Government approval was given for only a sixty-second display of the flashing neon tubes. A permanent switch-on was delayed until April, 1974.

The sculpture was less than enthusiastically received. Almost as soon as it was completed a campaign started to have it removed. It was described as a 'tangled and twisted monument to a drunken scaffolder' and became popularly known as the 'drunken pylon'. Others considered it a 'unique work of art'. Debate raged, but the fates seem to have conspired with its detractors from the outset. The lighting system rarely operated properly for any length of time, and attempts to repair the complicated electronic mechanism were unsuccessful and abandoned each time. The only person that might have been able to shed light on the problem — Dainton himself — had wisely moved to Australia.

The kinetic sculpture survived ten years, during which it almost never worked. It was removed in 1983, but all the parts were stored just in case the city ever wants it back.